Re-Membering with Goddess:

Healing the Patriarchal Perpetuation of Trauma

Girl God Books

Edited by Kay Turner,
Trista Hendren,
and Pat Daly

Cover Art by Kat Shaw

©2022 All Rights Reserved
ISBN: 978-82-93725-22-0

www.thegirlgod.com

Girl God Books

Just as I Am: Hymns Affirming the Divine Female

What is a Hermnal? It's the collective sigh of our ancestral Grandmothers. It's a means of drawing us closer together as Sisters. It is a compilation of songs that affirms our Sacredness, apart from Man, and assures us that we are Sovereign Beings and Creatrixes, too. And it is our Love Gift of Gratitude to Mama.

In Defiance of Oppression — The Legacy of Boudicca

An anthology that encapsulates the Spirit of the defiant warrior in a modern apathetic age. No longer will the voices of our sisters go unheard, as the ancient Goddesses return to the battlements, calling to ignite the spark within each and every one of us—to defy oppression wherever we find it, and stand together in solidarity.

Warrior Queen: Answering the Call of The Morrigan

A powerful anthology about the Irish Celtic Goddess. Each contributor brings The Morrigan to life with unique stories that invite readers to partake and inspire them to pen their own. Included are essays, poems, stories, chants, rituals, and art from dozens of story-tellers and artists from around the world, illustrating and recounting the many ways this powerful Goddess of war, death, and prophecy has changed their lives.

Willendorf's Legacy: The Sacred Body

Travel through time and discover a world where the fullness of women was both admired and deified. Reclaim your beautiful Goddess body through the rich pages of this powerful collection of art, poetry and essays celebrating our divine inheritance as daughters of Willendorf.

Original Resistance: Reclaiming Lilith, Reclaiming Ourselves

Through poetry, prose, incantation, prayer and imagery, women from all walks of life invite you to join them in the revolutionary act of claiming their place—of reclaiming themselves.

Re-visioning Medusa: from Monster to Divine Wisdom

A remarkable collection of essays, poems, and art by scholars who have researched Her, artists who have envisioned Her, and women who have known Her in their personal story. All have spoken with Her and share something of their communion in this anthology.

Inanna's Ascent: Reclaiming Female Power

Inanna's Ascent examines how females can rise from the underworld and reclaim their power, sovereignly expressed through poetry, prose and visual art. All contributors are extraordinary women in their own right, who have been through some difficult life lessons—and are brave enough to share their stories.

On the Wings of Isis: Reclaiming the Sovereignty of Auset

For centuries, women have lived, fought and died for their equality, independence and sovereignty. Originally known as Auset, the Egyptian Goddess Isis reveals such a path. Unfurl your wings and join an array of strong women who have embodied the Goddess of Ten Thousand Names to celebrate their authentic selves.

New Love: a reprogramming toolbox for undoing the knots

A powerful combination of emotional/spiritual techniques, art and inspiring words for women who wish to move away from patriarchal thought. *New Love* includes a mixture of compelling thoughts and suggestions for each day, along with a "toolbox" to help you change the parts of your life you want to heal.

How to Live Well Despite Capitalist Patriarchy

A book challenging societal assumptions to help women become stronger and break free of their chains.

The Girl God

A book for children young and old, celebrating the Divine Female by Trista Hendren. Magically illustrated by Elisabeth Slettnes with quotes from various faith traditions and feminist thinkers.

Complete list of Girl God publications at www.thegirlgod.com

"A trauma is a place where it becomes impossible to remain connected in and to the present moment. Trauma is a part of the human condition!

Healing is also a part of the human condition, and we have the capacity to transform difficult experiences into a wellspring of personal and spiritual power."

-Kimberley Ann Johnson

Dedicated to the Feminine and the body
in familial lines – healing and liberation
of past, present and future generations.

Table of Contents

Preface   1
Dr. Karen Ward

She Heals Me   4
Leticia Banegas

Re-Membering with Goddess   5
Trauma, Patriarchy and the Sacred Feminine
Kay Turner

A Note About Styles, Preferences and Names   11
Trista Hendren

Gathering Magic   14
Arna Baartz

Embodied Prayer   15
Kay Turner

Surviving "Traumarchy"   17
Sharon Smith

Oh Happy Day   27
Leticia Banegas

Finding Myself   28
Caroline Selles

Carolina   30
Caroline Selles

The Journey Home for this Divine Spark, Flying Free   31
D'vorah J. Grenn, Ph.D., Kohenet

Marjory -> Emma
Barbara Daughter
38

Motherline Re-Membering
Amber R Balk, Ph.D.
40

My Masterpiece
Tasha Curry
46

Medusa's Scream II
Claire Dorey
48

Where Does This Rage Come From?
Kaia Tingley
49

Streaming Cosmic Codes of Truth
Katrina Stadler
53

Still Finding My Way Home
Deborah A. Meyerriecks
54

The Way-Shower
Arlene Bailey
62

The Place of the Next Light
Arlene Bailey
63

Semilla
Arlene Bailey
67

Patriarchal Perpetuation of Trauma
Kay Turner
68

The Ghost Girl and The Goddess
Barbara O'Meara
70

The Ghost Girl and The Goddess
Barbara O'Meara
71

At the Heart of It 73
Arna Baartz

When My Heart Bursts Open I Can Weave 74
Songs of Blood and Love
Louise M Hewett

Withstanding the Storm 80
Arlene Bailey

Going In 84
Arna Baartz

Becoming the Breath Between 85
Arlene Bailey

Shapeshifting Trauma 93
Arlene Bailey

Vision Weaver 95
Arlene Bailey

When I Met the Goddess 96
Helena Anderson

Solstice Moon in a Land of Strife 99
Barbara O'Meara

Normalizing Abuse and Exploitation = Trauma 100
Anonymous

Red Saves Herself 107
Natalie Celine Couillard

Lineage of Mothers 108
Katrina Stadler

7 Ways Mothers Perpetuate Patriarchal Trauma in Their Daughters
Dawn Perez 109

The Wisdom in Feeling Devoured
Edy Pickens Levin 116

The Wisdom in Feeling Devoured and Waxing Crescent Transmutation: How Goddess Helps Me with Trauma
Edy Pickens Levin 117

Waxing Crescent Transmutation
Edy Pickens Levin 122

Do You Know Her
C. Abigail Pingree 123

Heal
Megan Welti 125

COLLAPSE, MOTHER
Dawn Perez 126

Revolutions of Defiant Ecstasy: Stealing Kali and Goddess Wisdom from the Primordial Wave of Feminism
Claire Dorey 128

I am Kali
Art and words by Kat Shaw 136

Sexual Abuse Healing Ritual
Annie Finch 139

Illuminatrix
Kat's Shaw 148

Facing My Trauma as a Female Leader within Patriarchy
Dr Lynne Sedgmore 149

Swimming a Witch
Donna Gerrard
156

I am Your Darkness
Words and Art by Kat Shaw
158

Healing Dreams
Trista Hendren
160

Reclaiming the Goddess
Barbara O'Meara
166

Dark Feminine ~ The Morrigan Speaks
Kathy Barenskie
167

The Morrigan
Kat Shaw
170

Holy Affliction
Lori Santo
171

Hecate
Kat Shaw
172

My Path to Hekate and Healing
Roxanne Rhoads
173

Mother of Medusa
Alorah Welti
178

Medusa's Scream III
Claire Dorey
180

Prisoner of War
Michelle Bear
181

Dark Lady
Words and Art by Kat Shaw
183

How Patriarchy Perpetuates Trauma   187
M^h

The Seed Blessing   197
Sue Ellen Parkinson

Healing from Patriarchy's Trauma Perpetuation   198
M^h

The Flood   204
Liz Darling

Who Am I?   205
M^h

The Seed   207
Arna Baartz

Embracing the Divine Feminine: How the Patriarchy   208
Perpetuates Trauma (and How to Heal from It)
Dr. Denise Renye

Tree of Life   215
Rebekah Myers

Wet Spring   216
Liz Darling

The Awakening of the Goddess   217
and the Healing of Patriarchal Trauma
Rev. Christian Ortiz, Ph.D.

Take it Back   226
Caroline Selles

Wild Flower (Vagina & Child)   227
Caroline Selles

The Goddess in the Garden:
Ode to My Divine Anger   228
Ellie Lieberman

Joyous Body/Universe   233
Alissa DeLaFuente

Burdensome Dance   234
C. Abigail Pingree

Remembering Goddess Through the Motherline: 235
Healing the Patriarchal Wound
Rita Shahi

The Healing Circle   244
Sue Ellen Parkinson

Can I Climb on Your Lap, Mama?   245
Sharon Smith

She Came from the Stars   249
Arlene Bailey

Hidden Gifts   250
Maureen Owen

The Serpent Was Actually God   260
Alorah Welti

Eve—Guided by Stars   261
Sue Ellen Parkinson

Sacred Call   262
Jen Abha

Las Curanderas   268
Sue Ellen Parkinson

A Prayer to the GODDESS MAYARI
from the Tagalog and Kapampangan
Mythologies of the Philippines
Dona Tumacder-Esteban   269

In the Beginning Was the Womb   271
Rebekah Myers

The Empty Womb   272
Liz Darling

The Healing Power of the Closing   273
of the Bones Ceremony
Rebekah Myers

Conclusion   287
Trista Hendren

Big Hug   290
Leticia Banegas

Additional Reading and Resources   291

List of Contributors   293

Acknowledgments   312

What's Next?   314

Trigger Warning:

This anthology includes graphic references relating to sexual abuse, rape, self-harm or violence that may cause psychological trauma, especially for those with anxiety or post-traumatic stress disorder. Please take good care of yourself as you work through this book.

Preface

Dr. Karen Ward

You are about to commence on a journey – an immram if you will, the Irish Gaelic for 'wonder voyage' of deep pain, visceral knowing, palpable shock, challenge and ultimately hope as you read the poignant words and gaze at the heartfelt images in this vital book.

There are not many books that come with a warning. This one does and it is a necessary addition. However unfortunately, you too may have also become inured to the stories told within. They are age old and weary, told time and time again. The difference is that now we have come to a new juncture in the world where a tipping point has been reached. A critical mass is waking up to this travesty that must stop not only for the future of humanity but now more than ever for Mother Earth. The Divine Feminine is rising.

Sensitively edited by Kay Louise Aldred, Trista Hendren and Pat Daly, this book is at the cutting edge of expressing cogently not only the past and where it has brought us to but most importantly a blueprint for the way forward. The contributors, both in prose and in image, convey sometimes eloquently and sometimes brutally how they not only survived but ultimately thrived against all the odds. The key is education, support, community to come to a place of being capable of the sacred personal work of healing. We have to, in the parlance of therapy, turn up for ourselves and literally 'do the work' otherwise we will remain mired in the binds of trauma for life.

As a Psychotherapist for many moons, I have been honoured to have worked with the survivors of institutional and parish abuse and the so called 'mother and baby homes', I have witnessed the debilitating effects of patriarchal trauma on both women and men. So deep that often these resilient people arrive at adulthood but never realise the extent of the damage that has rocked their core. And yet, the ones who do emerge to live not simply a good life but often an epic one have the same commonalities that are revealed in the pages of this book.

The healing stories begin with finding the right support. Not simply from others who are empathetic, but crucially those who are peers having been through similar situations themselves. Education is imperative to understand the effects of physical, mental, emotional, and sexual abuse and how insidious it is on growth, self-esteem and confidence. Next comes solace in nature with ritual and ceremony in community, the sisterhood circles bringing spirituality and the energetic in tandem with counselling and psychotherapy. Slowly, there is the tentative emergence of hard-won personal empowerment.

Towering over this labour of love are the archetypal energies of the Goddesses, waiting in the proverbial wings from ancient times to assist, sustain and encourage. This help from the unseen is evident in each story and painting pulsating off the pages in glorious vibrancy. The creative inspiration to self-heal. This is the gift of the Girl God. The key to the balance between the Divine Feminine and Divine Masculine both within each one of us and our women and menfolk. Gaia, Brigid, the Morrigan, Rhiannon, Macha, Shakti, Lilith, and the Crone to name but a few are pillars of strength and aid throughout. So often with their mythic stories mirroring those of the women writers and artists.

Gift this precious book to your friends, family, and colleagues and particularly your young adults both female and male. This needs to be discussed in our homes, streets, schools, and courts so that as a people we address this for once and for all. Enough!
When we Re-Member that we have a voice. When we call out disrespectful behaviour. When we band together in solidarity then the sea change that is required can happen globally and in the

major systems of our western world spreading out like the ripples in a pond to encompass everywhere.

Together we can change. Ní neart go cur le chéile. There is no strength without unity.

Dr Karen Ward
Dublin, Ireland

She Heals Me
Leticia Banegas

Re-Membering with Goddess:
Trauma, Patriarchy and the Sacred Feminine

Kay Louise Aldred

For the first 42 years of my life, I pinballed from one traumatic experience to another. It is understandable that I was initially relieved that there was a 'label' – Complex Trauma or C-PTSD – to explain my chaotic existence. In addition, it was liberating to learn that the plethora of symptoms I had previously or continued to experience – a long list which included shame, guilt and dissociation, chronic pain, fatigue and migraine, attachment issues, co-dependency, and self-destructive thoughts and behaviours – were not personal faults, weaknesses, or indeed punishments from 'God' for not being 'holy' or 'spiritual' or 'good enough,' but were instead by-products of nervous system dysregulation. Further understanding that the nervous system dysregulation was the result of the combination of generational dysfunction and patterns, in-utero and developmental trauma, adverse childhood experiences (known as ACE) and a catalogue of traumatic events and abusive relationships in adolescence and adulthood – was the catalyst for my journey out of victimhood.

I have experienced most categories of trauma and abuse, including familial suicide and alcoholism, parental emotional abuse and neglect, severe bullying, and physical assault at school, grooming and sexual assault, boundary violation and inappropriate conduct from a priest, financial and psychological abuse following divorce, and gaslighting and stonewalling by close family members. Now that I am aware of being born into a trauma landscape, I am able to forgive and be compassionate with myself. Acceptance has supported me to begin to forgive others. The predestined path of generational trauma is simultaneously no one's fault and everyone's responsibility to heal it.

The deeper I commit to recovery and journey ever further down the trauma rabbit hole, the more clearly I see the role patriarchy, religion and spirituality – 'ungrounded and inhumane 'spiritual' models that have been fostered by emotionally armoured, self-avoidant men' (Jeff Brown) – play in both causing, and perpetuating, the subsequent recurrence of it.

A hierarchical, vertical structure of 'power over' – the 'perfect,' ascended, all powerful and all-knowing, enlightened God-Deity-Guru to whom we silently pray-worship-venerate, putting our bodies into a controlled, paralysed genuflection or lotus position pose, hanging our heads in shame or awe, atoning for our 'humanness' and bodily based imperfections, begging to have our illusionary, sinful 'feelings' and emotions erased, undertaking practices to trigger 'transcendent' and 'blissful' i.e., dissociated states – are all the exact opposite of what needs to be cultivated to move on from trauma. Spiritual bypassing – 'avoidance in holy drag' (Robert Augustus Masters) – is an addictive behaviour, and one I still must keep in check myself. It can keep us netted in the search to be 'saved' by a means, power, or person external to ourselves and it was a compulsion which perpetuated my disempowerment, victimhood, and avoidance of self-responsibility, blocking the resolution of the trauma in my nervous system for so long.

The traumatic experience of societal decencies and cultural conditioning (Irene Lyon) which we have little collective awareness of, manifests as 'good, quiet and proper' behaviour. Twinned with patriarchal abuse, women are traumatised and then blamed both for it – and the symptoms they exhibit because of the unresolved trauma responses in their system. This is the ultimate toxic double bind and here are just some examples from my own life:

- **'Be good'** My soul-led, creative, and intuitive little girl was tamed into a good, compliant, high-achieving academic, who 'controlled' the urges and desire to 'break free' with an eating disorder. Consequence: blamed and labelled mentally ill.

- **'Be quiet'** As a separated woman I was told by my soon-to-be ex-husband not to 'rock the boat' or dispute his request for shared care of our children, which he made for his own financial benefit. My instinct was that if I did not agree to his demand, he would take me to court, and put our children through a custody battle. I agreed to his wishes even though my intuition (later proven to be correct), was that this was not in the best interests of our children. The event triggered the symptoms of chronic migraine and pain. Consequence: blamed and told symptoms were psychosomatic, 'all in the mind' and 'of the ego.'

- **'Be proper'** As a young woman, recently graduated from university, I was 'punished' (her words) by my mother, who took a deliberate overdose and self-harmed because I spent time caring for my suicidal father when he was on weekend leave from a mental health unit. My mother told me in the hospital emergency department she had done it because I had chosen 'him over her' that afternoon. This incident fanned the flames of social phobia and chronic anxiety, and further obliterated my already fragile self-confidence. The event elicited terror of my own voice, boundaries, and choices but also further amplified the lack of safety I felt in my family of origin, and with other women. Consequence: blamed and told I needed to toughen up, that my mother was suffering, and that my recollection of events was false.

As I write this and reflect, I now acknowledge that the final scenario is the 'worst' traumatic injury and attachment rupture I have sustained. This narrative demonstrates the ongoing frequent occurrence amongst individuals and groups of women – mothers and daughters included – who are both ensnared within and perpetuating the toxic historical patterns of patriarchy – traumatising and abusing each other. I doubt I am alone in experiencing and recognising this and I wonder if all women right now were to commit fully to breaking down these toxic inter-generational feminine energetics and dynamics – the patriarchy would finally crumble.

When I became conscious of my own internal misogyny and patriarchy, I set the intention to do inner work and restore the healthy feminine within myself. This has been painful, but for me was an essential part of resolving trauma. Thankfully, this has facilitated some beautiful connections in my life with many wise women, along with strengthening my link to the sacredness of the feminine. The nudge that this was a vital part of trauma healing came early. In one of my initial EMDR (eye movement desensitization and reprocessing) sessions I announced to the clinical psychologist during an eye movement sequence – that 'Divine Mother is here.' The creativity and ingenuity of the psychologist to accept and 'work' with this archetypical celestial intervention, was so enabling that the rewiring of my wounded 'mother attachment' was extraordinary and a great blessing. I was 43 years old, and it was the first time I had experienced and felt a sense of safe and sacred feminine energy, despite having been immersed in theology, religion, and spirituality my entire life. The cloaked figure of light arrived to take my traumatised inner child away from the event she was perpetually reexperiencing, placing her under her 'wing' and into safety. This 'being' is an archetypical aspect of light Goddess in the form that I now identify as Mother Mary or Kuan Yin. She was my psyche's lifeline out of trauma, patriarchy and the fear, disgust, and mistrust of woman, the feminine and the divine.

The imprinting of the frequency of the sacred feminine within my mind and body in that session has grown stronger through commitment and nurturance. I tune in over and over again, to receive the guidance of where to go next – whom to speak to, what to read, what to study, what to eat, how to be, when to rest.

A complete overhaul of my own and family's life was initiated that day, as the blueprint and innocence of my inner child was restored. When you heal trauma, you do so for past, present, and future generations. It is not work for the faint-hearted. Relationship dynamics, behaviours, thoughts, identity, and life purpose are all detoxed, recalibrated, realigned. Boundaries are negotiated and set, then renegotiated and set again. In committing to resolving trauma I have had to finally and fully incarnate, embody my complete and messy humanness, get up close and personal with my shadow and body sensations, and FEEL and contain everything at its strongest amplification – pain, anger, fear, hatred, despair. It was in this 'underworld' that my psyche met and was mentored by the archetypical aspects of dark Goddess in her many forms – Black Madonna, Kali, Morrigan, and Jaguar, to name a few. These dark and formidable energies and role models have walked me back along ancestral lines (deep into the collective wounding) and journeyed me to past lives, reminding me of the current 'mission' many of my contemporaries also have – to clear out and exorcise the violence, cruelty, harm, denigration, rape, and violation of the feminine, the body and the earth. Through the personal healing of any one of us there is a restoration of life, a voice, embodiment.

I am, you are, we are, the sacred feminine – one in the same – and I own this fully. By continually re-claiming, re-membering and re-connecting myself as Goddess, answerable only to my own inner gnosis, I heal and resolve trauma. What I evoke, pray to, petition, is all inside of me. I trust my own wisdom. I move. I nurture my body. I commune through pleasure. I see my bodily sensations and emotions as messengers carrying wisdom. I feel and express a full range of emotions. I root my energy system into the earthly womb of Gaia and the cosmic womb of Sophia and receive eros, inspiration and lifeforce. I embrace all the aspects, energies and archetypes of Goddess that I am. I am beginning to trust and lean into my newly found circles of sisters for reflection, companionship, and love.

And this is my journey in its infancy. I have a lot more processing to do around shame and vulnerability, being seen and heard, fawning and fitting in. Nevertheless, as I advocate for the unification of the sacred and mundane, I have set the intention and called upon the activation of the energetics of self-leadership and self-sovereignty of the sacredness and feminine wisdom of my own and my family's DNA and energy field, whilst knowing and trusting fully, that it is already done.

A Note on Styles, Preferences and Names

Trista Hendren

Re-Membering with Goddess contains a variety of writing styles from people around the world. Various forms of English are included in this anthology and we chose to keep spellings of the writers' place of origin to honor/honour each individual's unique voice.

It was the expressed intent of the editors to not police standards of citation, transliteration and formatting. Contributors have determined which citation style, italicization policy and transliteration system to adopt in their pieces. The resulting diversity is a reflection of the diverse academic fields, genres and personal expressions represented by the authors.[1]

People often get caught up on whether we say *Goddess* or *Girl God* or *Divine Female* vs. *Divine Feminine*. Personally, I try to just listen to what the speaker is trying to say. The fact remains that few of us were privileged with a woman-affirming education—and we all have a lot of time to make up for. Let's all be gentle with each other through that process.

The late Carol P. Christ wrote:

> "To name God in oneself, or to speak the word 'Goddess' again after many centuries of silence is to reverse age-old patterns of thinking in which male power and female subordination are viewed as the norm... Though Goddess has yet to become a familiar name, the word is being spoken more and more often. And many women feel chills of recognition as they hear the word, which names the

---

1   This paragraph is borrowed and adapted with love from *A Jihad for Justice: Honoring the Work and Life of Amina Wadud*. Edited by Kecia Ali, Juliane Hammer and Laury Silvers.

11

legitimacy and beneficence of female power. The reemergence of the Goddess in contemporary culture gathers together many of the themes of women's spiritual quest. It is a new naming of women's power, women's bodies, women's feelings of connection to nature, and women's bonds with each other."[2]

We hope to bring healing through this anthology through the re-membering and naming of Goddess in all Her forms.

Please take good care of yourself as you read through the pages of this book. You may find some passages triggering. Self-care, movement, and deep rest will be important tools as you work through this anthology.

You will notice that we have included more art in this anthology than in those previously published. This was intentional on our part. We ordered several proof copies of this book to ensure that it was not too 'heavy.' We want people to finish this book feeling hopeful. I have found art particularly healing in my own life. My home is covered in woman-affirming Goddess art that has been foundational in my healing and journey to self-love. If you find a particular writing triggering, flip through the book until you find an image that is comforting to you.

None of us gets through life without some sort of trauma. Life is traumatic in and of itself. As Brené Brown wrote:

> "Everyone has a story or a struggle that will break your heart. And, if we're really paying attention, most people have a story that will bring us to our knees."[3]

---

2   Christ, Carol P. *Diving Deep & Surfacing: Women Writers on Spiritual Quest.* Beacon Press; Revised 3rd edition, 1995.
3   Brown, Brené "Everyone Has a Story." Posted on her blog on June 07, 2018. https://brenebrown.com/articles/2018/06/07/everyone-has-a-story/

Our life's work is to heal.

If you find that a particular writing doesn't sit well with you, please feel free to use the Al-Anon suggestion: "Take what you like, leave the rest!" That said, if there aren't at least several pieces that challenge you, we have not done our job here.

Toko-pa Turner wrote:

> "True healing is an unglamorous process of living into the long lengths of pain. Forging forward in the darkness. Holding the tension between hoping to get well and the acceptance of what is happening. Tendering a devotion to the task of recovery, while being willing to live with the permanence of a wound; befriending it with an earnest tenacity to meet it where it lives without pushing our agenda upon it. But here's the paradox: you must accept what is happening while also keeping the heart pulsing towards your becoming, however slow and whispering it may be."[4]

May we all find such a healing through the words, art and rituals in this anthology.

---

4 Turner, Toko-pa. "Pain: The Un-welcome Guest." AUG 13, 2019.
   https://toko-pa.com/2019/08/13/pain-the-unwelcome-guest/

Gathering Magic

Arna Baartz

Embodied Prayer

Kay Louise Aldred

Hands together. Eyes closed. 'Our Father, who art in Heaven...'

This is how I was taught to pray in Sunday School, and then at Primary School, where every assembly also ended with a pious repetition of the Lord's Prayer. Rote recitation of the biblical words, in sing song intonation (actually, thinking about, we collectively narrated this prayer in the same rhythm and tone as our times tables!). Week after week we droned on, with the additional command, as we got older, to be absolutely still.

I became numb to it all – the words, the meaning, the concept. So, one day, as I neared the end of this age range, I decided to sway during the prayer. The rhythm had become anchored into my body, and I wanted to move with it. Feel it. Play with it. I no longer had any cognition 'online' with regards to the sentiment of the words. At 10 years old I still didn't really understand the trespass bit anyway. I just 'knew' I had to move the beat of our collective voices through my body.

So, I did. And this is how I began...
'Our father' – sway to the right.
'Who art in heaven' – sway to the left.
'Hallowed be thy name' – spiral.

The spiral movement took hold and became the main theme for the rest of the process – even though I really wanted to create a swooshing too much into fountain movement, raising my arms above my head, but even at the time thought this might be a bit too much.

It turned out it was all a bit too much. I was publicly shamed, immediately after the prayer was completed – in front of the entire assembly hall, the whole school. I was chastised and told my movement was disrespectful and that I should know better at the age I was, etc., etc.

That was the day, as a child, when I lost all contact with the Divine Feminine.

Surviving "Traumarchy"
Sharon Smith

I grew up traumatized by Patriarchy. I didn't know it at the time, but now I can see clearly the negative effects this androcentric Dominator System had on my body, my mind, and my soul as a girl growing into womanhood during the '60s and '70s.

My first experience was physical abuse at the hands of my mother who had been, herself, the victim of child abuse perpetrated by her own mother who told her (as she beat her), "Girls are no goddamned good! Only boys are good!" She was the only daughter in a family of eight children. And she was the only one who ever got beaten.

This abusive domination of my mother undoubtedly traumatized her. But it was also an early and destructive imprint upon her "love map," and it dictated what kind of mother she would be to her own daughter.

And then I was born, the second child and only girl of three children.

The first beating I recall was when I was still in a highchair. I remember this event clearly. Pain has a way of etching itself upon body and mind. My mom had sat me in the highchair and given me a bowl of jello. I was expecting the little wiggly cubes she usually cut it into, but this time she had whipped the dessert into a frothy substance that I didn't recognize. So, I pushed it away to let her know I didn't want it. Unfortunately, I pushed the bowl a little too hard and it went crashing to the floor, spilling the frothy jello all over the linoleum.

My mom was furious! She got one of dad's belts, and then she grabbed me by the arms and yanked me out of the highchair. She lashed the belt across my back and buttocks hard... with the buckle end. I remember screaming in pain. But she kept on whipping me till my body shook. Finally, when she stopped, the pain had spread itself into a total body numbness. That was my first memory of dissociating from my body.

My mom apparently had internalized the patriarchal belief that "girls are no goddamned good; only boys are good" which had been beaten into her. And she taught me in return.

"Traumarchy"—that's a word coined by Meera Atkinson, author of the book, Traumata. She describes it thus: "the way patriarchy perpetuates trauma, making it 'inherently traumatic' and giving rise to a multitude of sufferings and strife." My life has been a struggle to overcome traumarchy in more than just physical abuse.

At age three I also suffered child sexual abuse at the hands of an uncle, who digitally raped me... and then threatened to kill me if I told anyone. I was so frightened that I began to cocoon myself under the covers in my bed each night, thinking I'd be "hidden and safe" if he came through my bedroom window. I also began to bed wet, which had the unfortunate consequence of angering my mother, which resulted in more beatings.

But the trauma didn't end there.

Throughout my youth, I was subjected to the groping hands of neighborhood boys and even some of my own male cousins. One teenage cousin asked me to go into the woods with him so we could "fuck." I was too young at the time to know what "fuck" meant, but it didn't seem like anything I wanted to do, so I said "No" and ran home. The boys always got away with their harassment and assaults, because—and who hasn't heard this one?—"boys will be boys!"

Sad thing is, the boys who groped my body (without my permission, of course)—sometimes grabbing my breasts or my crotch or pinching my behind—talked dirty about me and spread lies and rumors, so, of course, I was called a "slut" and a "whore." Funny, because I hadn't even "fucked" yet. But that didn't matter. Boys could say whatever they wanted to shame and blame girls. And girls just had to keep their mouths shut.

Traumarchy: Patriarchal trauma. It left me feeling ashamed and dirty. And I hadn't really done anything worthy of it. Except be born a girl.

After high school, I, like many girls of that time period, got married. I had met my husband in my senior year (he had already graduated and was working as a stock boy at a local grocery store) and we had "fallen in love." We got engaged during that final year of school and "tied the knot" (wonderful saying, no?) in August of 1972. The "honeymoon" didn't last long.

I found myself going from an abusive home-life to an abusive marriage. Except this time, the abuse wasn't physical. It was mental and emotional abuse and neglect. And, in many ways, it hurt far worse.

For most of my 28-years with this man, I was neglected and mentally/verbally abused. For instance, while I was very pregnant with his child—belly large and protruding—he seemed to get a kick out of focusing on my weight gain. On one occasion (at church, no less), he saw me walking toward him and exclaimed aloud while our church friends looked on: "Hey, Hey, Hey: Here comes Faaaaaat Albert!" in the cartoon voice. I wanted to disappear through the cracks in the floor of that "sanctuary." He thought it was "funny;" I found it humiliating and demeaning. He laughed... I went into the bathroom, locked the door, and cried.

After about the third year of our marriage, my husband stopped getting me cards for any occasion—not even my birthday or Mother's Day (although I had two beautiful daughters with him). And no gifts either. Not even at Christmas. I continued to buy him cards and gifts, and I strived to be a "Proverbs 31 Woman," according to my Fundamentalist Christian beliefs. I was a stay-at-home Mom and did my utmost to make that man feel like the King of His Castle, as we were taught Christian wives should.

But nothing worked. And, for a time, I kept blaming myself, kept working harder, kept giving and doing and being what I thought *he* needed—forget what *I* needed. That obviously didn't matter. Because under patriarchal teaching, all that truly matters is the man—his wants and needs, his thoughts and opinions.

Then in 1993, I discovered my husband had been having an affair with a woman from his place of employment. It had been going on for at least a year, possibly more. That was the ultimate slap in the face. Yet, still I persevered, thinking that "saving my marriage" was the right and dutiful thing to do.

At first, my efforts seemed to be paying off: my husband quit his job and went to work for a company in another village, closer to our church. We decided to try to sell our home and relocate to a place in between this new job and our church. But a few months in, my husband was terminated, due to lack of seniority and a troubled economy. He immediately went back to his former place of employment... and his "girlfriend." The affair took up where it had left off.

I found them together in our home one Sunday afternoon, when I drove twenty-two miles from a neighboring village, where our youngest daughter had starred that weekend in a "Best of Broadway" theater production, thinking he might want to attend the after-show cast party. First thing I noticed, upon returning home, was a strange car parked out front where I normally parked my car. *It might be someone visiting a neighbor,* I told myself... but I had this nagging feeling in the pit of my stomach. (Sisters, always pay attention to that "nagging feeling.") When I went inside and called his name, I heard him come running down the stairs. He met me in the kitchen. I noticed right away he seemed edgy, nervous.

After hemming and hawing a bit, making small talk, he said, "You need to know that *Becky[5] is upstairs."

"What?" I said, my stomach sinking.

"She came by last night to pick up a piece of jewelry I had fixed for her and, when she went to leave, her car wouldn't start. It was storming out and she had nowhere to go, so I told her she could stay here."

I could feel my blood beginning to boil. I looked him in the eye, parted my bangs and said, "Does it look like I have 'STUPID' tattooed on my forehead? Get her out of my house NOW!" I had had it. Something in me finally broke.

He disappeared and a few minutes later I heard them coming down the stairs, mumbling together, and then the front door opened and closed. I waited until I heard the car leave before I walked into the living room, where my husband stood, looking out the window. "How could you do this to me again?" I asked through teary eyes.

He turned to me and said, "Because I'm a man and I have my needs!"

I had a small glass of orange juice in my hands. I threw it at him.

---

5 Becky is not her real name, but because she is a victim of spousal abuse in her first marriage and a woman wounded by Patriarchy herself, I choose to protect her privacy.

And left.

Man's needs. Patriarchy: It's always about a Man's needs. With no thought whatsoever about what a Woman needs—like self-worth and respect and some genuine love.

I knew then that it was over. I wanted a divorce. But first, I went to the elder women in my church and told them my story. I expected they would rally around me in "sisterly support." But instead, this is what I got:

> "You can't leave your husband! That's not God's will. God hates divorce. You have to go home and try harder to be a more submissive and loving wife, so that he doesn't feel the need to look outside the marriage for his comfort."

I was stunned. They blamed ME. It was ALL on me. *My* fault he cheated on me. *My* fault he was abusive and neglectful. *I* had to work harder.

I went home that night totally disillusioned, dispirited, and deeply depressed. After the girls went to bed, I stood in the kitchen, washing the supper dishes. At one point I picked up a sharp carving knife and thought how easy it would be to slit my wrist and just bleed out on the floor. That was how depressed and desperate I was feeling. Even my own God wasn't on my side. I lifted my eyes heavenward and said, "God, if this is all you have for me, then I don't want it!" And I meant it.

I didn't take my life (obviously), thanks to my two daughters. I couldn't leave them with a selfish, neglectful, and abusive man. They'd never really had a father, and I couldn't leave them without a mother too. They deserved better.

So I prayed—not to the "Father God" I had spent so long

worshiping and serving. I was done with him. Instead, I prayed to whoever would hear me and offer me some help... and some real hope.

I needed to grow a backbone and finally stand up for myself. So, that night, I packed my husband's clothing and personal items and set them by the front door. When he came home from work the next morning and saw the suitcases and bags he said, "What's all this?"

"It's your stuff!" I replied.

"Well, what am I supposed to do with it?" he asked.

"I don't care," I said. "Take it to your mother's. Take it to Becky's. Just take it and GO!"

He left in a huff. But as soon as he was gone, a huge weight lifted off my shoulders. A couple of weeks later, my youngest daughter said to me, "You know, Mom, the house seems so much lighter and feels so much better now that Dad isn't here." She paused a moment and continued, "You should have kicked Dad out years ago!"

I looked at her, stunned by her comment. "I stayed with your father all of those years for you and your sister," I explained.

My daughter looked me in the eye: "Mom, really, you didn't do us any favors!"

The next few years were difficult as my husband did his best to make my life miserable, Although he knew I was still homeschooling our youngest daughter, and that, should I have wanted to get a job, I couldn't see to drive at night and our little country town in upstate New York had no jobs to offer a woman with only a high school education and no real job experience outside of the home (which, of course, didn't count), he stopped paying any of the bills, including the mortgage. This put me in a real bind.

When I took him to court to try to get some spousal support, the "judge"—a man I later discovered was Becky's cousin—said there was no reason I couldn't get a job, so he denied me any support.

Again, the System is rooted and founded upon Patriarchy, and often run by men for men. The fact that my husband's name was still on the deed didn't matter; the fact that I was finishing up our daughter's schooling didn't matter. The fact that I couldn't see to drive after dark didn't matter. The fact that finding any jobs nearby didn't matter. Once more, it was *all on ME*.

This is how Patriarchy traumatizes women—it forces us to be dependent upon men, and when men aren't present in our lives, it penalizes us for trying to stand on our own. Patriarchy continues to try and knock us off our feet and keep us down. Patriarchal religion wants us to be under the dominion of men, subject to men's wants and desires... and God forbid if we balk against that system! We'll get penalized by the patriarchal politics of the patriarchal judicial system. We're screwed no matter which way we turn.

That's why we must be tough, and why we have to get involved. But we can do nothing so long as we are left traumatized by Traumarchy.

We have to heal from that trauma first. How can we do that? Here's what worked for me:

We heal through our Sisters. Through groups of women who have survived and learned how to thrive, despite the pervasiveness of patriarchal thought in our society. I began to heal when I

24

discovered a wonderful Women's Retreat in the Pacific Northwest, after moving there in 2012. Twice a year for five-and-a-half years (Spring and Autumn) I attended these retreats that used dream imagery, empowering Goddess myths, song & dance, creativity through writing and artwork, and opportunities to share our personal stories in Circle Time to facilitate healing. The love and support of that beautiful Circle of Sisters was very much the healing balm I needed. The ability to tell my story in a safe place—and not be judged or condemned—was cathartic. All the lessons I learned during those retreats have become a part of my self-healing work, as well.

Healing from patriarchal trauma takes time. We have to unlearn a lot of lies and misinformation that was taught to us, whether knowingly or unknowingly, whether innocently or purposefully, by our parents, our school systems and our society in general—through politics, religion, capitalist economics, and through TV and movies, magazines and advertisements. We've been inundated by Patriarchy most of our lives, so undoing the damage is not going to be a "quick-fix."

There are a lot of wonderful books on the market that can help women understand the root of Patriarchy and how it became the dominant system in much of the world today. I would suggest googling these books, getting copies, and reading and studying them. There are also many empowering books created to help women love themselves and discover their sovereignty as unique and sacred beings (like Girl God Books!). These can be great tools for building self-confidence and in developing spiritual practices that reintroduce the Divine Feminine (Goddess-consciousness), rather than the patriarchal "Father God" concept that has kept women in a "lesser-than" submissive role for several millennia.

We can overcome Patriarchy's trauma—"Traumarchy"—no matter the damage it has done to our self-esteem or our self-worth. But it takes courage and determination... and a lot of hard work to heal our wounded selves. I know because I've lived it. I nearly lost my life to it. But I am not a victim; I'm a survivor—and my life, today, is happy, productive, and peaceful.

I've gone from Wounded to Wonderful... and, Sisters, so can you!

Oh Happy Day

Leticia Banegas

Finding Myself

Caroline Selles

I open the box of puzzle pieces that are my pain.
As I sort through the jumble of jagged bleeding pieces, I notice
My illusions
My faults
My failures
My trauma.

The edges form the suit of armor so familiar, comfortable, and
suffocating.
The colors are muted and faded.
The design prescribed by others
My family
My peers
My rapist
My newsfeed.

Edges no longer match.
Pieces no longer fit.
The picture on the box, so attractive and acceptable to others,
The image I am told I should want to form seems
Grotesque
Artificial
Offensive
Unacceptable to me.

One by one, I lovingly scrape off the blood and reshape the pieces.
I add vibrant colors
Of laughter
Of tears
Of dancing
Of truth.

The suit of armor is replaced by a blanket, warm, cozy, comforting and fluid.
I allow the tenderness to mold, not an image, but a feeling. A feeling
Of love
Of belonging
Of connection
Of safety.

I am finding myself, one piece at a time.

Carolina

Caroline Selles

The Journey Home for this Divine Spark, Flying Free

D'vorah J. Grenn, Ph.D., Kohenet

When did I take my last – or my first – breath that was safe from patriarchy, that wasn't influenced, dominated by, enveloped in the damaging structures and language of a patriarchal culture?

When did I begin to pray freely, openly, unencumbered, unafraid, un-self-conscious, without shards and shreds of imposed guilt and patriarchy running through my consciousness?

How insistent and constant were the voices of white patriarchs informing my image of G'd and keeping the Goddess hidden from me, putting forth instead only the image of an old, judgmental white man with long white beard, not the vibrant female whose embodied, protective energy can be felt through Shekhinah, Ishtar, Lilith, Anat? Her Presence is so alive in Kali and Durga, in the tree, wind and water goddesses Asherah, Yemaya/Olokun, Oshun, Oya, there can be no mistaking Her power. Now I see Her everywhere, Her essence in the coast live oak, Japanese black pine and Nature-sculpted piece of giant redwood in our garden.

It is said in the Talmud that when two people study Torah together, it is as if the Shekhinah – often called "the female face of G'd" in Judaism – is between them. Not G'd, but Shekhinah AS G'd, a secret well-kept from me until I was in my late 40's. I was so excited to learn this, and so later viewed with disbelief that She had once again been erased, in an image projected onto one long New York museum wall; it said G'd, not Shekhinah in the quote. I viewed it with outrage, knowing that few people would automatically think of G'd as representing a female energy.

In starting this article, several questions swirled through my head: which trauma do I write about? How many of them? Didn't Goddess come into play to help me cope with all of them, even unbeknownst to me? Did She save me from being raped in Golden Gate Park when I was a 17-year-old virgin? As I thought about how to begin, I felt such an essay would entail my remembering all the traumas and so might be too dangerous to attempt. But my subconscious knew I had to write what I could.

As I speak these words aloud, thinking through how the process might go, I remember another attempted rape in an empty hotel bathroom in California at age 23 and two date rapes. Do I include the date rapes? I didn't even have language for them until long after the fact. I hadn't classified them as violent – though they were forceful – perhaps because I was partly in shock or denial, and partly blamed myself for getting into compromising situations. I'm not sure rape was a word I used to describe them until much later.

After these events, I continued on with my life. But what went missing was my full voice, the ability to recognize the incidents for what they were and their impact on me. Perhaps I lost a small piece of me after each incident.

All these acts left for a time a soul-killing residue. Our culture teaches us not to see certain things, or to live with them, to be silent for fear of consequences from ostracization to violent blowback. Our own guilt, shame, self-accusation, internalized oppression do a good job of concretizing these silences; that itself is part of the patriarchal design. It's emotionally and spiritually lethal in its effectiveness... hiding in the shadows yet making itself felt in changes to our personality, in shutting down trust in our own intuitive alert systems so that we can't recognize or name what's been done to us. After years of conditioning both societal and personal, we start believing the lies: "Oh, I must've overreacted, must be remembering this wrong. Oh, I'm sure he didn't mean it. Oh Oh Oh..." until we have talked ourselves out of our own sense, collaborated in stripping away our essence until sometimes there's nothing left of *us*, or just a shell, a silhouette of who we were.

Patriarchal systems perpetuate trauma by convincing us something we've gone through "wasn't that bad" or didn't compare with another woman's more visible or constant injuries. We now recognize this as minimizing our pain, ignoring the reality/validity of our experience, or as gaslighting to make us question our own perceptions, even our sanity.

I didn't find the Goddess and Her healing presence and properties until my husband died — and even more fully 21 months later, after watching a lover die in front of me. The deaths were a compound trauma and put me in a state of spiritual emergency, which in retrospect I feel was Goddess's way of getting through to me as I walked through life in a workaholic oblivion. I was cracked open and threw myself headlong into Her open arms without quite knowing why. I just knew I was hungry to know more about this Goddess I'd read about after the deaths; She felt like much more than just the female face of G'd, or one of the benign goddesses we learned about in school, Greco-Roman co-optations of the earlier powerful ancient Mesopotamian and African deities.

Through reading Jean Shinoda Bolen's *Goddesses in Everywoman,* Vicki Noble's *Shakti* Woman and Clarissa Pinkola Estés' *Women Who Run with the Wolves,* I started to understand what had happened to me, what parts of me had been slowly stripped away or killed off with great intent, parts that could return now that I was free and on my own. Not needing anyone's approval or fearing anyone's punitive response, I became consumed with Her study and Her worship, and began writing liturgy. I wrote my first piece in 1999, "Inanna-Lilith-Shekhinah," later published in my *Talking to Goddess* anthology. She became an organizing principle, and more: part of my very lifeblood, a vital affirmation of all the things I was and am. I realized how many parts of Me were never allowed to surface, never given support or encouragement because of the imposition of patriarchal values, mores, expectations.

Slowly, those missing pieces of Self came back together. Large pieces of my heart and spirit returned once I was able to identify patriarchy and learned that I was not alone in suffering its deleterious effects. Amazingly, unless I blocked it out, I didn't remember knowing the word before hearing Monica Sjöö speak about dismantling patriarchy at a Women's Spirituality Festival produced by Z Budapest. At that festival, I found a new world. The words spoken, dances danced, rituals offered stirred new connections in me; the ecstatic feeling I experienced was true embodiment, all my own and in unfamiliar but deep relationship with other women, and Her. As I moved to the beats of a mother drum, I saw women being in their wildness in ways I'd never witnessed. The weekend struck a chord so deep I moved straight into a trajectory of Women's Spirituality graduate studies: doctoral exploration into women's rituals within a new extended family, Lemba Jews in South Africa, and discovery of a new thealogy grounded in the Sacred Feminine, the female/androgynous deities of Yoruba/Ifa West African traditions and my own ancient and contemporary Jewish lineage.

These learnings resulted in my braiding together those traditions and a feminist spirituality as my spiritual practice, one I embraced initially with guilt, and later with great joy and a deep knowing. Such woven practices are rich and can be antidotes to patriarchal dictates since they allow for adaptations of the male-dominated organized religions in which many of us were raised.

How did Goddess help me move through the worst of my trauma? By bringing me into women's community and guiding me into a course of study that infused me, enhanced and fed me far better than the most lavish dinner, with far greater rewards. I knew I could turn to Her in times of great need or utter despair. Just knowing She *existed* gave me a more alive connection to Divinity, both Hers and mine, and the freedom to surrender without fear of being subsumed. That was something I'd never been able to do before; indeed, I had rebelled against it, given that the liturgy in services I had attended spoke to us as children of a male parent, the male G'd. I have no doubt it was that kind of language that helped alienate me from my Judaism for so long. Even now when I try to be a bit more inclusive and not leave the male out entirely, it is hard. It's not that She never gets angry. Of course, She does; at times She has a great deal of righteous rage. But unlike the male god, Her anger gives *me* permission to have rage, both for myself and on behalf of others. That is why archetypal figures such as Lilith, Inanna, Kali and Anat are such compelling, important models.

I can talk about Goddess as healer, as good listener, as compassionate Mother, as unconditional love, in ways that I could never imagine the male G'd to be, since that god is often portrayed and perceived as jealous, vengeful, punitive, all-powerful and omnipresent, cold and distant, issuing "Thou shalt nots" far better than He could listen or comfort.

IN CONCLUSION

Among the most obvious answers to the question posed by this volume, "How does patriarchy perpetuate trauma?" are these: Through sexist, misogynistic or white supremacist threads running through most commercials and ads, news stories, films, TV and radio shows; across social media, the gaming world, sports; on campuses throughout the country; in most organized religions undergirding their dogma, liturgy, daily office and organizational policies; in corporations, in politics, in our laws and in our lack of the laws that are much needed to fight androcentric biases; in the medical and hospitality industries, and in the majority of our institutions.

35

Where does patriarchy NOT perpetuate trauma might be a better question. It succeeds by self-replicating and continues by erasing our history, marginalizing women and many men, building strong walls around itself through sabotaging, defunding, and destroying people, institutions and social justice movements fighting the status quo to create a more balanced world. Patriarchy also perpetuates intergenerational trauma by, for example, insisting in some states that slavery and America's systemic racism *not* be taught in schools!

In patriarchal religions, one is often taught that to get angry at or question G'd – or clergy – is unacceptable; it's well-known this mindset has led to sexual and spiritual abuses. With Goddess at the helm, I feel invited to be relational, allowing for argument, questioning, thealogical discourse.

When men are viewed as god/s because "G'd is male" as Mary Daly said, patriarchy also perpetuates trauma by supporting abusive intimate relationships, frequently not prosecuting men, or awarding them minimal sentences that make mockery of their crimes.

Goddess Spirituality can give us many healing tools, including finding forgiveness and compassion for ourselves. It offers "thealogy as embodiment" as Carol Christ wrote. Both embodied and arts-based techniques are invaluable. When my colleagues Dianne Jenett, Judy Grahn and I co-directed a Women's Spirituality MA program, we included a somatics-based course, Embodied Spirituality, and Art as Sacred Practice. Many students found these modalities to be healing. And certainly, finding a spirituality grounded in and by the Goddess has helped many heal from grief and move through major life transitions.

The very male-dominated system which creates and often supports traumatic situations – from rape to domestic violence and more – cannot possibly heal itself. "The master's tools will never dismantle the master's house," poet and womanist/civil rights activist Audre Lorde pointed out. It's up to us to end this damaging system NOW. As June Jordan and others have said, We are the ones we've been waiting for.

Marjory -> Emma
Barbara Daughter

This painting imagines and images Marjory Stoneman Douglas as a role model for X (Emma) González, both of whom fought for social and environmental justice. Marjory Stoneman Douglas's dedication to the preservation of the Florida Everglades is represented, as is Gonzalez's stand against gun violence. This art also honors the 17 victims of gun violence at Marjory Stoneman Douglas High School. Both male pattern violence and capitalism-driven disregard for our natural world are key components of the patriarchal world we live within, and fight against.

Motherline Re-Membering

Amber R Balk, Ph.D.

Incarnating into a home devoid of goddess, I was born in 1982 into a fundamentalist Christian family in rural Tennessee to a Native American mother and a father of English, Irish, and Welsh descent. Not only was there was no goddess at home but none in the entire town, except perhaps a brief glimpse of her in the Catholic church, a fact my Pentecostal mother considered repulsive and heretical. I was not allowed to go near the Catholic church, not that I felt particularly called to visit.

Both parents were disconnected in various ways from ancestral roots, but it was more explicit and malicious on my mother's end. Her dark skin, obsidian eyes, and raven-blue-black hair she regarded as an abomination, a curse. Ever strategic, she chose my father for his pale skin, blond hair, and blue eyes. Being Native American was taboo in our household. Right up there with the goddess. Right up there with *pagan* (generally pronounced with a spat). Right up there with The Devil. These things were bad and would earn you a nonstop, one-way ticket to eternity in hell.

"Mama, what should I put on the tests for race? White? Native American? Other?" Truly perplexed, I asked this after my first day of standardized testing in elementary school.

Spontaneous combustion. "YOU ARE WHITE!!!" she growled.

"Oh. Hmmm... [glances at brown arm, looks at mother's obvious non-whiteness] Okay, but..."

"But nothing." End of conversation.

Thankfully, I have always been rebellious and headstrong. I knew something was terribly off in her words and actions, but it would take many years to gain understanding. Re-membering would be largely a solo journey. I tried to find answers everywhere but ran into endless locked doors. I did not realize this lack of external answers was habitually turning me to look inward instead. I did not think I had any answers. With time, I realized this inherent self-mistrust was inaccurate and unnecessary. Like internalized racism, internalized disempowerment serves to break one down from the inside out. When the weapon is seeded as a self-activating force through generations of oppression, hatred, and abuse, it is particularly insidious. Challenging to see, much less root out. But it is possible. Dismemberment helps, but re-membering is essential.

The following story is told in bits and pieces of lived experience, woven together through blood, breath, prayer, and ritual. The demanding journey required much: 20+ years of Jungian analysis, countless hours weeping and screaming in Holotropic Breathwork sessions, lots of dreamwork, late night conversations with wonderful friends, notebook after notebook of journaling, a degree in women's spirituality, another degree in transpersonal psychology, and countless prayers and ceremonies. I share my story with the hope and intention that it will serve others on parallel paths of re-membering.

2006. Dismemberment commences. I cut myself out of my parents' home. The choice clear, either become a submissive housewife like my mother or shape myself into an accomplished professional. A westward call whispered its beckoning since I was about eight years old. With heaves of daring determination and a willingness to sever ties and leave all my friends and family, I finally arrive in California. Initially, it is an ecstatic self-homecoming. I enter doctoral studies as a perfectionistic, driven 24-year-old. Focused. Ambitious. Competitive. And perhaps narrow-minded, which I translate as hyper-fixated on lofty goals. With certainty, I am confident this is an ideal approach to life. A good girl, I swallow my patriarchal lessons whole.

Dismemberment continues as aspirations and drive are stripped away. In my first year of graduate studies, it creeps in slowly and overtakes me in a disorienting fog that I never saw coming. Nothing works. My research ideas are rejected (however, I am offered the option of pursuing a male professor's research ideas instead, which I politely decline and then find myself increasingly ostracized and unsupported). My spark fades. Before long, I am struggling for direction, frantically treading water. This quickly develops into a full-blown attempt to keep my head above tumultuous waves, and when this fails, I sink to the bottom, swallowed by the depths of a dark night of the soul. These clichéd metaphors are intended to sidestep the boring and mundane details of daily lackluster life. For a feisty, ambitious young woman under the impression that she is fierce, independent, and on a mission, this layer of dismemberment is probably the most painful. Before this point in my development, I thought I had escaped patriarchal trauma, but it slowly begins to reveal itself through the stripping.

In desperation I sign up for a Lakota-style vision quest in Mt. Shasta, hoping for clarity but also longing for a taste of Native American perspective, so lacking from my Native American life. My ancestors are Choctaw and likely of other southeastern tribal affiliations—we do not really know. I usually identify myself as "a descendant of the southeastern peoples of the Mighty Mississippi River Valley." The Mississippi is my mother goddess. Lakota culture is quite different, in background, cosmology, and region, but the teachings I receive are much better than the nothing my mother dishes out.

After months of preparation, both physically and spiritually, I spend four days and three nights camped on Mt. Shasta beneath tall pines with little more than prayer ties and courage. On the third day, I am meditating in a pleasantly receptive state of mind. A hummingbird hovers overhead, and ripples of iridescent energy course through my body. I ask questions in my mind and hear

42

immediate responses. After playing around with this newfound entertaining ability, I summon my most important query: "Will I be a good psychologist? I mean, will I make a difference in the world?" Instead of an immediate response, there is a long pause. Wind snakes through the trees. A squirrel barks. I am about to give up waiting when the words come: "You... will be a wonderful mother." I roll my eyes and huff. This is the last thing I want to hear.

The schism. Where did this disdain for *mother* originate? I trace it to my first birthday, thanks to the video my father takes that day. My mother had disappeared for days. She returns on my birthday looking pained and exhausted and brandishing a colicky newborn. I am disheveled and confused. In need of reassurance, I desperately reach toward her and attempt to crawl into her lap. I hit an electric fence, unknowingly pushing against a fresh wound, concealed beneath her clothing, a long vertical line spanning her abdomen. Reacting to the intense pain, she pushes me away. Reacting to the intense pain, I push her away. The blueprint of our dynamic is cast, repeated endlessly in the years to come.

I vehemently reject my mother—everything about her. She is weak. Afraid of my father, she timidly caters to his demands. She does not pursue a career but instead labors on housework and recruits my sister and I to do the same (but not my brothers). She watches soap operas and binges potato chips. Preachy and insisting on reading the Bible aloud, she fills the space with yucky feelings that I later understand are shame and guilt, but they are not mine. Terrified of natural childbirth, she has four c-sections. By choice. She finds breastfeeding vulgar and emphasizes that sex is sinful. She has gifts and can see auras, but the topic is especially taboo. She fears being inherently evil, a message conveyed by her father and the church patriarchs of her childhood.

The interesting thing—also off the table for discussion—is that my mother is given away at birth in 1952 and spends her first six months in an orphanage in Oklahoma. The social climate of that time and place is decidedly racist, dominated by white, god-fearing, Christian men. The US government and various religious groups actively try weeding out remaining natives in numerous ways—forced sterilization, assimilation, Christianization, outlawing spiritual practices, banning languages, enforcing boarding schools, and coercing adoption into white families, just to name a few. We do not know the specifics of my mother's birth, but after years of re-membering, I am certain these circumstances shape what happened. She is adopted into a white Christian household. Just as I reject my mother, she rejects her mother, who had rejected her at birth.

2008. Vera Cruz. Hugely pregnant, a dream rolls through one night. I know I am in Veracruz (a place I have never visited in the waking world), walking along a coastline. I see something at the water's edge and run to get a closer look. A beautiful gigantic snake! As I realize this, a big wave comes in, mixing water over my legs and the snake. I try not to panic. The wave recedes as another comes in. I am caught between the two waves, tugged by earthshaking forces pulling in opposite directions.

This dream comes back to me weeks later as I lie strapped to a cross-shaped surgery table. My worst nightmare comes true as I am forced to have an emergency c-section after laboring at home with a midwife for 36 hours without progression. Womb horizontally sliced; my daughter is pulled from my protective body. I have no choice but to surrender. This layer of dismemberment brings immense physical pain, but it serves as an important catalyst. Although I continue to view her fear of vaginal birth as tragic and revealing, it becomes impossible to view my mother as weak for choosing four c-sections. Only a warrior could willingly agree to such a thing.

This realization softens the hardness I harbor towards my mother. We become friends. I wear my daughter against my body for six months, attempting to remedy the amount of time my mother spent orphaned and un-held. My mother is the wave going out, my daughter the incoming wave. I did not know it when I had the dream, but *Vera Cruz* means True Cross, a significant detail in my process of re-membering. I always disliked the cross symbol in Christianity, but as a universal symbol reflecting the union of opposites and a convergence of the four directions into sacred center, I can resonate and navigate by that. True Cross turns out to be a place of surrender and reckoning, of immanence and transcendence, of paradox meeting and merging. True Cross brings me home to my feminine power as I heal the scars of cuts drawn across multidimensional layers of my being.

Vera Cruz is a goddess who helps me re-member during a time of literal, figurative, and extreme emotional dismemberment. The goddess comes through my fiery motherline warrior spirit. She speaks in dream, in song, in love and aversion, in intuition, and sometimes in poetry. She speaks in my daughter's fiercely independent voice. She speaks in prayers for my mother, who has now passed. She is the Mighty Mississippi. She is everywhere. She was always there.

My story is one version of reclaiming the feminine power that has been stifled, shoved into nooks and crannies, hidden, denied, feared, violated, and desecrated across the planet and across a long span of time. We are living in an age when such power can be excavated, revived, renewed, and enlivened. I am part of that. My mother and daughter are part of that unfolding, as are you. And when I think of it like that, the fire of warrior women across the ages ignites in my blood. I feel the drumbeat pulsing, and I know the pain and suffering are not in vain. Though the journey at times seems solitary and daunting, we are interconnected. I have deep faith in what is unfolding on a bigger, collective scale. Individual re-membering is a doorway to healing the fractures of patriarchal trauma. We find it in our mothers and daughters. We find it swirling within our sacred places of Vera Cruz.

My Masterpiece
Tasha Curry

I'm angry.
Angry that I overcompensate for it; Fight to forget it.
Angry that I'm still crying.
Angry that I push away my lover because of it;
Flip out on my kids when I think of it.
Angry my friends don't all know.
Angry that I felt so humiliated, alone... betrayed.
I was used.

Angry that out of shame and horror I didn't recognize it... until it was too late.
Angry that smoke drowns my pain and blackens my lungs.
Angry that I have forsaken my true self: no more choir, dance, theater or poems.
I miss art.
I was a masterpiece.

Angry there's no single release; No more innocence.
Angry that it's eaten at my joy.
I. See. Red.
Like the red light shining down on me, awakened from my blackout.
I'm angry that night didn't stay black.
I was a black masterpiece.

Angry I briefly saw a handful of guys, handling my naked body.
Angry I had to scream "no!"
Angry I had to slap!
They didn't stop. Or did they?
Angry I blacked out again and couldn't tell you.
Angry my story has already been told, spread like a lie in the wind.
A lie that was easier for me to uphold than the truth...

I was a breezy masterpiece.

I'm angry the only way to not be angry is to cry.
Angry I'm still angry.
Angry that I must keep grieving
So. Many. More. Steps.
Will I forgive those that stepped on me?
This, I must keep grieving.
A survivor must grieve.
Angry that I'm called a survivor... classic...
I'm a classic masterpiece.

Medusa's Scream II

Claire Dorey

Where Does This Rage Come From?

Kaia Tingley

There has been a deep trauma.

To all of us.

In all of us.

By all of us.

Against divinity herself.

We have been the victims. We have been the perpetrators too.

I do not know the name. I cannot describe the agony. But I bear witness to it nonetheless. It is real. It happened and we can no longer afford to pretend that it did not.

I don't have to know what happened. I don't have to feel it all over again. But the bedrock of truth is unyielding. A steady place to rest, if even for just the briefest moment.

There is no blame, actually. It just is *a thing*. A block in the vibration of infinity. A hiccup in the grand scheme of things.

But it was painful all the same. Deeply painful in the way of giving birth. The ring of fire.

THIS is where the rage comes from.

Deep within us on a primal level.

The trauma happened a very long time ago. When some people discovered that they could rule others through fear and power.

Since domination became the foundational zeitgeist of human progress. Since we started trying to put an infinite, linear progression on top of the cyclical rhythm of nature.

Since we decided a global economy (and its flow of profit to the few scions of power at the top) was more important than the very skin of the earth, and the stability of our families.

We will continue to pass on the block in the darkness of unawareness for so long as we continue to flee towards what we perceive as safety rather than embrace the light of truth. Our physical gender in this lifetime is irrelevant to this process.

The trauma shaped us. It brought us collectively to the point that we are experiencing right here. Right now.

Do you see the edge? Do you feel it?

Forgiveness is not a logical thing.

It is not something the mind can decide, or religion can dictate must happen.

It is not something to be broken down, analyzed, or understood.

It is not even a one-time thing.

Forgiveness is a mystery. She's the sister of Eros herself. We aren't built to understand. That's ok.

She's the muse Dona Mwiria speaks of seducing. The harbinger of pleasure. The very essence of what it means to be alive and to know it.

She calls us back to beauty. She calls us to the bright blue sky and the perfect beauty of the clouds chasing one another home. She sings the siren song of coherence in a world gone mad. She is the ground under our bare feet and the wind in our hair.

Do you hear her singing?

Her voice is beautiful despite the trauma she's endured. Her seeds will always sprout, even after they've been crushed and burned and smeared into nothing. They will still grow if we can imagine that love still exists.

She's more powerful than anyone can possibly imagine. The definition of juicy. Forgiveness, dressed in her modest clothes, holds the secret of the future in her small, carefully cupped hands.

She offers us a cup of calming tea.

Do we dare to allow her softness again?

It seems imprudent, but...

I take the cup of tea.

The world has always seemed to be trying to crush me into a tight little square space when my nature has demanded flow. Get a job! says Amanda Palmer. I feel that...

But I crave circular spaces. White walls and dark wooden floors. Healthy dark green plants, soft breezes, wide-open skies. Cool pools in the dark evening and the enchanted sound of music sung in low harmonious voices. A warm hand on the small of my back. Permission granted to be as I am. No different.

I've struggled with structure imposed upon form, and form animated by flow, in a never ending cycle. Haven't you?

Is this, at its heart, a problem of perception? Or is it the law of the Tao?

Must there always be pain? Is the pain the necessary precursor to beauty?

Is this just the way it was supposed to be?

I don't feel in my heart that it is. But I release the attachment to knowing.

I release the story that I am supposed to be someone else in order to have the right to know this. That I should suffer more. Enough with the suffering!

If these words come through me to you, then so be it! It is up to you now to decide whether or not to receive them. I will never take that from you.

Contrast doesn't have to mean control.

We *can* learn to allow for fluidity within a structure, can't we? Coherence is after all just an adjustment to the frequencies of previously negating waveforms.

The inexorable pull of the tide brings me back to the place of stillness. The space between the inhale and the exhale. The exhale and the inhale.

There is beauty in both sides. The union of the opposites could be just fine.

We have been given the choice. It is upon us. Do you see it?

All I can do is bear witness.

I am content with the choice I have made.

I sip my tea and smile.

Streaming Cosmic Codes of Truth
Katrina Stadler

Still Finding My Way Home

Deborah A. Meyerriecks

I was raped, therefore no longer a virgin. So, the Church of My Parents, and those who follow it, called me a sinner. I conceived a child as a consequence of that rape. So, the Church of My Parents and those who follow it, called me a sinner for having sex and becoming pregnant out of wedlock. I was taken in shame by my mother to have the abortion my grandmother paid for in secret, so the Church of My Parents, and those who follow it, called me a sinner.

More specifically, a murderer. Whore, temptress, murderer, sinner. I was twelve years old and a freshman in high school.

In my earliest memories, I recall my father touching me as though I was his property. He called it love and told me to keep "our" secret. I learned to shut down, shut off, and not feel. I was beaten for not responding to him the way he wanted. When I finally summoned my courage, found my voice, and told my mother, I was beaten for 'lying.'

Another sin. Not mine. None of them mine. You see, she feared losing child support from my father. She feared I would cause him to withhold those necessary funds. She feared how it would look to her father and the trouble it would create.

I've grown up sensitive to the reaction of other people for similarly toxic reasons. I stopped eating things I had to chew because when my jaw clicked and popped, my mother would chastise me for disturbing the people dining with us. I couldn't control it. I was told to go eat in another room. When I took it upon myself to eat elsewhere, I was labeled "rude" and "antisocial." After all, we have visitors, or we were guests and my behavior is a reflection on her. My comfort was never a consideration. I let them know once, only once, that when my jaw popped it was quite painful. "Deborah, what do you want me to do about it? Just stop doing it."

I learned to never mention it again. I learned to break food into the tiniest of bites, soak it in milk, sip water with it. When I was tired, literally tired and sore, from trying to eat something particularly difficult she would say I was full from drinking too much. That I'd be hungry again soon but there won't be anything for me unless I clean my plate. Don't give anyone an opportunity to call her a bad parent. Don't let them think she didn't feed us enough.

My relationship with Popa, my mother's father, was wonderful. Still, I saw the subtle ways the rules of patriarchy governed our family. Children and young women are meant to be quiet, obedient, and complacent. Do well so there would be things to celebrate and brag about but be quiet else-wise. Be seen but not heard.

When my grandmother and my mother brought me for my abortion, I had to lie. A lot. I had to tell my family (or whoever asked) that I was recovering from an ovarian cyst removal. I had to cover for my grandmother spending the money on me and my "dilemma." All these years later it is not lost on me that my lie had to be based in female "weakness."

I had already been sick for weeks. Many doctor's appointments and tests later, a nurse failed to check the under sixteen box for the blood work. I was pregnant. I'd already had an upper and lower GI series. They tell you the solution you have to choke down isn't that bad. I threw it up and was labeled a "difficult girl."

The following summer, between my freshman and sophomore years in high school, I'd been staying with my aunt and uncle during their work week as a live-in babysitter. She was finishing her degree by taking night classes. My aunt would pick me up Monday night on her way home from work. Friday night on his way into work, my uncle would drive me back to my mother's house.

It started when I was still young. No place was home. It was always someone else's house and I just lived there. Not because that's what I was told but because how I felt. I'm still trying to find my way home. I learned there is a word that means longing for a home you've never been to and hope you will recognize when you get there. I do not find it reassuring that such a word even has to exist. I find no comfort knowing others feel homeless too.

During that summer, my aunt became upset with me when she was subjected to her husband's "grossed out" sensitivities. She said we (herself included) did not use the (covered) wastebasket in the bathroom (next to the toilet) to dispose of sanitary napkins each month. Didn't my mother teach me anything? According to my aunt at that moment, my mother wasn't practical but lazy if she let us use the wastebasket in the bathroom for those. "Where anyone could see what was in there!" I swear, she visibly shivered at the thought.

We would be subjected to the toxic, verbal diarrhea that spewed effortlessly from his mouth all month long. You wouldn't dare confront him. His house. He's king. If you don't like it, don't come here. While I never hear such terrible things from my Popa, he did maintain a 'my house-my rules,' take it or leave it dynamic. Not 'their' house. 'His.' Wives and children were conveniently left out.

My aunt paid me a nice sum. It lifted some financial strain off my mother. One less mouth to feed during the week and one less load of laundry because I'd wash my clothes before going back on Friday night. Enough cash to buy my own school supplies and clothes in the fall. Some pocket money for bus fare and lunch for a while. I even managed a couple of movies and ice cream with friends that summer but often, they paid for me.

When I was old enough to stay away, I was again accused of rude, anti-social behavior. I was the reason family ties were stretching thin to breaking loose.

And that's exactly what I was doing. I was breaking free.

Free from fathers who touch daughters, enforcing secrecy with threats of beatings or victimizing a younger sister. Free from mothers who would beat their daughters for lying, which meant speaking a truth they did not want to hear. In particular, a truth that threatened her financial security.

I remember seeing parts of the Ted Danson movie "Something About Amelia" that was playing on the television in the living room as I did my homework at the dining room table. Everyone was saying how awful, how terrible... how anyone who did such a thing should at the very least have their hands cut off. I could have jumped out of my skin. I settled for jumping up out of my chair.

"That was what my father did to me! Will you accept it's wrong now?"

I was told to be quiet, stop being dramatic, stop being ridiculous. My mother cried that I believed she would let such a thing happen. Her denial. It cut even deeper this time.

As I developed, family friends with the honorary title of Uncle would pass through the house. Whenever they could get away with it, I would be cornered, touched, groped. They would trace the curve of my ass and my new breasts, and I was expected to let them. Pretend nothing is happening. Eventually they'll stop. Kisses on cheeks became awful kisses on my mouth while pressed up against the wall in my bedroom, or in an empty corner of the house. They slipped their hands in my panties and pressed my hand against their penis through their pants.

Don't tell, don't say anything. I watched them leave twenty-dollar bills next to the kitchen cups where my mother would keep her cash.

"Don't tell, don't say anything" my mother would say as she watched them bring their children to play with my sister in our yard and put grocery bags on our kitchen table that provided the night's shared meal and filled the refrigerator for us for the rest of the week. Don't tell, don't say anything. What would your grandfather think? You'll embarrass them and they won't come back. Who would your sisters play with? My mother, being close with their wives, didn't want to lose her friends.

Don't tell, don't tell, don't tell. I told. Nothing good happened. I learned to be silent. I learned not to feel. I learned I only matter for what I can either do for others or let be done to me. There's an invisible power we give them when we don't tell. As a child you are powerless if no one will listen or worse, silences you.

Slowly though, I learned that there was someone listening.

Since my teenage years, I've been a self-proclaimed witch. Initially, I rejected the notion of any deity. If gods existed and allowed this to happen to children, then even the gods were evil. I felt safe in Nature. I would roam the forest near my mother's home. In Queens, (NYC) we have a lovely spot called Forest Park. It's absolutely magickal.

I would ride the subway to Rockaway Beach and walk the surf at night, any time of the year. With the Sun on my face, I had access to all the elements. Earth, Air, Fire, Water.

I was a tree hugger whom the trees would hug back. Grounding, calming hugs. Water, whether ocean, river, or lake, held and supported and carried me. The joy of a child feeling weightless in her mother's arms. Rain and breeze gave soft caresses without restraining. Wind blew away the cobwebs and refreshed thought and feeling. Heavy downpours could wash everything away. Air listened to my whispers and songs. Sun's Fire shown down on my face when I could tolerate it like the beaming pride of parents we read about and see in other families.

I turned inward and eventually learned Spirit. I found a strength that had always been there. I put a capital "N" on Nature and called her my church. I came to know Gaia, Mother Earth. Later while exploring my Irish roots, I learned of Rhiannon and her story of tolerating men's ridiculous power over women with incredible strength. She had commitments to honor. She could have left at any time. She chose to use her strength, to stay and fulfill her commitments.

I don't remember not being suicidal. How beautiful it would have been to go to sleep and never have to wake up again to this world, where fathers hurt their daughters and this patriarchal system allows it? I had younger sisters to protect. I didn't know why but I needed to stay. As an act of defiance, maybe. I never intended to become a mother myself. The Patriarchal Trauma Curse would end with me.

When I found out I was pregnant with my son, I had just escaped an abusive relationship with his biological father. I was told right off the bat that I should go back to him.

No. Absolutely not. I was still recovering from being thrown down a flight of stairs. What mother would send their daughter back to that? One who was taught her value was based on her ability to raise obedient, seen but not heard children.

The next day while speaking with a trusted friend, she asked if I'd decided to keep the baby. "I haven't," I said. I was young, had a low income and unreliable job, and not the best living situation at my mother's place. I told her I would look into adoption agencies if I couldn't make it work. She said that she meant abortion and to call her because she would never let me do that alone. When her words sunk in, I vomited on my own shoes. I was fiercely pro-choice. I still am. There was never a doubt after that, my baby was going to be born. I was going to be a mom. My son was born healthy and loved.

Four years later I married the man who would be the father of my daughter. She was born soon after my son's 6th birthday. Two years later, when his abuse became rampant, I left him and moved back in with my mother. She was recovering from a stroke; I was working full time. My youngest sister was still living there with her 2-year-old daughter. It seemed like a good arrangement for all of us.

My daughter and son were exposed to levels of toxicity that I feared were inescapable. Then my mother died. After her death, I was able to sell her house. That set my Dynamic Duo and I up with a small apartment. I paid off my mother's debt and I gave the rest to my sister who used it as a down payment on her own house.

In the following years my Dynamic Duo witnessed me distance myself from toxic family situations. I didn't break the curse by not having children. I broke it though my children. My son is compassionate and strong. He acknowledges his personal issues and chooses to work on them and heal rather than bleed on those around him. My daughter is strong, outspoken, and courageous. She has learned to recognize a toxic situation and remove herself from it. No one will ever coerce her into something she isn't comfortable with. No one will ever make her keep promises. No one will silence her truth.

In recent years I've learned the names of more goddesses.

Goddesses of War and Death, who teach us to fight for what we need and to stand up for ourselves. Goddesses who don't put us in harm's way, but if we are willing, they give us strength in battle and guard our backs while we fight. Goddesses, I would learn who were with me all along. Offering me their outreached hands. Enabling me to get up and stand firm in my truth. Offering me their swords. Goddesses who were reminding me of my strength. The strength I always had and that's why I survived and learned to thrive. In spite of—and not because of trauma.

Funny things happen on the road back from War. During our rebirth after the death of our old self identity, we learn to love ourselves. We learn that we don't need any love that comes with toxic strings. Not from fathers or mothers. Not from any of the others who claim to love you, want you, need you, yet always hurt you. Blaming you for being hurt. If they cry martyr because you called them out on their toxic behavior, run them through with your sword and walk away. You've got this. I've got this. Goddess sees us and is standing ready to give us that sword the moment we realize we were always strong enough to wield our own strength and power.

I'm strong enough in my healing that I can now send love up the family line to my mother. She needs it most, I think. She wasn't a bad person. She loved us. She was trapped, depressed, and isolated emotionally. She did the best she could with what she was taught to expect out of life. I've learned to forgive that her best wasn't good enough. I'd like to believe she tried. I'd like to believe that somehow through my own healing, the strength of my daughter with her ability to love without fear of control or oppression or pain, that my mother is smiling. I hope she found her way home and is healing with her Mother Goddess from the wounds of toxic patriarchy that she was blind to see she perpetuated. I hope, like me, she found her voice. The voice I ensured my daughter never had taken away. I hope she is already home. I'm still finding my way.

I offer this generational cure with love.

The Way-Shower

Arlene Bailey

The Place of the Next Light

Arlene Bailey

I've held it all in,
all the hopes and dreams,
the cries of despair...
held it all in until today.

Until today when I felt this net of despair
fall over me choking me, strangling me,
blocking the air so I couldn't breathe.

I saw her tears as we locked eyes
and knew in our hearts that the soul,
my soul, is now on the auction block.

I keened for hours in the woods.
Keened for what has already been lost...
what is currently being lost...
what is potentially still to come.

I made altars and offered ritual.
Screamed guttural prayers
to the Mother of All
that enough is enough!

Still the tears came,
but the keening vocals grew quieter
as I had no more to give.
Even the crows and hawks went silent
sensing a pause of sacred reverence.

Where to now I asked?
Where do you want to go, She replied?
I don't know.

I'm tired and disillusioned
and want to crawl into my cave
and have the Old Ones wrap
their arms around me.

Then that is what you do.
But before you go, you offer...

One last prayer to the dreamtime.
One last offering of hope planted
in these darkening times.
One last ritual of rebirth that even now
gestates in the womb of the Mother,
that gestates in the womb and heart of you.
One last offering given with all the fight of
the Warrioress that lives within you.

Then you rest and wait and trust the
Ancient Ones to guide you through
to the place of the next light.

What if there is no more light, I ask?
Only darkness and evil?

Evil has and will always exist She said,
but so does the light.
Find that place and know
the light always returns.
Perhaps dimmed,
Perhaps brightly illuminative,
but the light always returns.

Until that time...

Rest so you are able to still build
altars to new possibilities and
keen over the bones of what is lost.
Rest until that time you can
give voice to the both/and.

Until that time, vision and dream and
allow the Ancestors to wrap you in
ancient wisdom, ancient knowing
as you embrace the sacred dark.

Until such time the light rises like
the woman you are, blazing and
empowered and screaming like the
Banshee taking no prisoners,
as you build altars to the sacred new.

As you remember you are a
Daughter of the Cosmic Mother.
Daughter of the As Above, So Below
who aspires to the heights and
plunges the depths as She
walks between the worlds.

So, scream like the Banshee
and keen over the bones.
Light the fires of ritual
and offer prayers to the
Ancient and Future ones.

Though the world may change and,
perhaps, not in the way you desire
while grief and trauma shift and morph,
you will survive and even prosper
IF you remember who you are
and the power you hold.

Remember...

She who is the Great Mother Goddess,
Warrioress and Ancestor and more.
She who is Ancient Bone Woman
and She who is yet to be re-born.

Remember...

She who will always hold and inform you.

Remember...

You are you own Way-Shower and need
only look for the place of the next light.

Remember.
Remember.
Remember.

The Place of the Next Light by Arlene Bailey, ©2020, 2021

Semilla

Arlene Bailey

*Semilla is Spanish for Seed. As such, She represents the potential in everything and everyone to transmute what is dead or dying into new life... to create beauty where only sadness and dross once lived.

Art and Words by Arlene Bailey, ©2020, 2021

Patriarchal Perpetuation of Trauma

Kay Louise Aldred

Too much. Sit still. Too slow.
You're wrong! I'm right!
Be grateful for all they did for you.
Take the Pill. Any pill.

You're unstable. Your depression is back.
Write it down to get it off your chest.
That's not how we do things.
Take a paracetamol.

Just breathe and let it pass.
Stop doodling.
That's the wrong answer.
Have a hysterectomy.

I think you need to see a professional.
Write in full sentences.
We haven't got time for questions (or feelings).
Botox? Or at least a cream.

It's too late to report it.
It's your word against his now.
Memory is subjective.
There's no forensic evidence.

You'll understand if I don't agree.
Or disagree, or challenge them,
Or support you.
They'll come after me if I do.

Don't feel.
Don't feel your body.
Don't feel.
Don't feel and express.

God is male.
Meditation heals. Still your mind.
Ascend. Out. Up. Leave.
Higher states of consciousness are where it's at.

Don't feel.

The Ghost Girl and The Goddess
Barbara O'Meara

The Ghost Girl and The Goddess

Barbara O'Meara

That which the Ghost Girl had prophesied
Came to pass as signified
A rarified starfish child was tossed aside
Pure Innocence taken and brutalized
Senseless loss unjustified
A dark red stain became vaporized
Kith and kin catastrophized, terrified
Broken hearts treated and tranquilized
And I, the Ghost Girl, grew petrified
Making my way submissively, stupefied
My cold blood drained and jellified
In an aftermath forever stigmatized
But
The Goddess would not abandon me
Persistently rising to rescue personally
I was not forsaken in my selective isolation
She felt my pain, my considerable desperation
Divine feminine healing emanated towards me
Casting light on shadows of what was meant to be
Walking wounded woman was actively set free
To claim her place as elemental healer of energy
Originated void became filled with lightness
Probing, penetrating the cavernous darkness
Packing in with natures gauze
Powerful and potent as ever was
Infused with a salty ocean brew
Droplets of tincture swirling around
The astringent salve cleansing with no abound
Polishing ossified bones with comfort and care
Releasing compression and stagnant air
Vital life forces re awoken

A stirring of heart remnants, resting unbroken
I who had journeyed unaccompanied in grief
Unbeknownst to my marginalized state
SHE would never permit such a destructive thief
To steal my existence as yet incomplete
Intuitively tracking that which had not died
A tiny remainder still unblemished and alive
She emancipated me from my own self-exile
Observing my wound but detached from all trouble
Transcendence was permitted from life's long struggle
Reclusive tendencies alleviated towards dissolution
Evaporated into the ether with newfound resolution
An eradication of all forms of alienation
Discontinued forever with rekindling and reclamation
Of love and hope and divine feminine adoration
I honor my female gifts with self deification
Bestowed on me, a once living Ghostess
I am now the embodiment of my divine female hostess
I dedicate my life with unquestionable devotion
To the Glory of the Goddess who re-set me in motion

At the Heart of It

Arna Baartz

When My Heart Bursts Open
I Can Weave Songs of Blood and Love

Louise M Hewett

'When I was twenty-seven I had a baby. He came through a mist or a fire, a presence that was like a roar in me, from the mystic water into the uncompromising air. I believed he was perfect, an epiphany of the divine, in that instant... triggering a process of rebirth within myself.'

These words are from the opening paragraph of an essay titled 'Waking to Myself' which I wrote in the autumn of 1994, about a year after my son was born. The essay was subsequently published in the Winter 1994 edition of *SoundingSophia*, a publication for Sophia, 'a feminist spirituality centre concerned with the development of women's spirituality, justice, and care for the environment'[6] in Cumberland Park, South Australia. The following year I wrote another piece, 'Born Again Woman,' published in the Spring 1995 edition, beginning: *'Once upon a time just recently I became a Feminist. Prior to that I was slumbering. I know this because I've woken up.'* The waking up was intimately entwined with the birthing of my first child, an inwardly focused as much as an outwardly and materially focused journey into actively embodying the primal relationship, the tri-spiral relationship of mother, child, and environment. The process of waking up was painful, like a birth, although some of the pain was due to trauma, old and new: dominator parenting and socialisation, the patriarchal religious prescription of being. Sexual violation, rape.

During my first pregnancy I wrestled with a sense that my child would be taken away from me by an unnamed presence, a force of admonishment, of shame which at that time I felt to be located in my mother. My mother was the woman who had journeyed in a

---

6   *SoundingSophia* No. 3, Winter 1994.

similar way, the reason I had life at all. But there were conflicts and hurts given to me by my mother, and what child is canny about what not to receive, what is useful? It was only later as I learned more about women's history, feminist thought, and the clever art of shaping questions that I understood the sleight of hand: traumatise generations of daughters, blame mothers, and render invisible the foreground abusers. It certainly took conscious effort to navigate a journey away from mother-blame with constructive compassion, a tiring road as I began to mother my own child, desperate to avoid repeating the destructive and constrictive parenting techniques I knew as my own conditioning.

In that essay from 1994 I also wrote, 'trauma was a catalyst.' I'll pause to briefly explain the particular trauma I was referring to at that time. After my first birth journey in May 1993 I merged easily and whole-heartedly with the sense of myself grounded as mother/motherer, albeit needing to learn everything, and to discard what I now knew as inappropriate. It was a complex initiatory journey, endings and beginnings interwoven in obvious and yet subtle ways. Mother-infant bonding was immediate and for five days I experienced ecstatic states, trance-like mother-son unity, the discomfort and profound revelation of breastfeeding: a rebirth of *me*.

On the sixth day after the birth, I was told my son had a heart murmur, a hole in his heart. That it couldn't be ignored. I didn't really grasp what it meant at that time, but this was his *heart*, the centre of his life and another part of my own heart! Three months later I was told by a cardiologist that due to the size and nature of the problem he would die, whether in his first year or during early childhood. It was certain. He had a congenital, ventricular septal defect. VSD for short. It was considered large, and fatal. *Fatal*. He would need surgery before the age of six months.[7]

---

7   I remember sitting utterly devastated in the car after seeing the cardiologist, the song 'Heartbeat' was playing on the car radio. *Heartbeat* (Tainai Kaiki II), 1992, Ryuichi Sakamoto, David Sylvian and Ingrid Chavez. Words: David Sylvian, Ryuichi Sakamoto; Music: Arto Lindsay, David Sylvian, Ryuichi

The power of this knowledge, this awakening initiating experience, ruptured *my* psychic heart. And then, heart ruptured, I realised how heartbroken I'd been for so long, for most of my life really: unaware, underdeveloped, timid, violated, unheard, insignificant, unreal... wounded in body-mind. I knew there were others in far more terrible circumstances than I was, that I should be grateful, that my life was an absolute dream compared to the lives of some... but it was the cardiologist who'd expressly told me not to do that. He said I was *allowed* to grieve, allowed to feel. He said that I couldn't compare my experience to anyone else's, not in that way. My own experience was mine and it was real. I had to engage with it. I think they were some of the wisest words ever given to me. And so then, *then*, I *could* feel, and I could choose what to prioritise and where to place my creativity. Then, I experienced what it was *to love*, to remain open and raw to life, to my own needs as well as the needs of my son. Then, I was shown the depth and potential of the responsible practise of maternal consciousness. And it hurt so very much.

If it was such a good thing, why did it hurt? Because the blossoming and the weaving, the creative birthing of my relational consciousness was happening simultaneous to the rupturing, the decomposing, the shattering of the child raised and socialised in patriarchy and patriarchal heterosexist femininity. The realisations of my developing feminist consciousness were slow at first, and I can of course say now that as the years rolled by, they became faster, and glaringly intense, foundation and flow facilitating ever more understanding. And amidst this creative process, the "everyday" traumas of living in dominator patriarchy were exposed along with experiences I'd purposefully buried in chambers not meant for living things. It was inevitable, I suppose, that when the excavations began old shit would emerge in the attire of neglect.

Sakamoto; Vocals: David Sylvian, Ingrid Chavez. 1992 Virgin Records
<https://www.youtube.com/watch?v=XtvTDuTbPhU>

My son's VSD and my heartbreak was an intersection where many threads coincidentally met, and a quickening process occurred. What were these threads, in general? At twelve years old I'd dipped into an Eastern mysticism via a book I picked up in the local supermarket, thinking I was rejecting the basic ideas and concepts of being that permeated my culture and my personal experience. Given the dark looks from parents, alienation from other teenagers, I quickly realised this was all very unacceptable. And so, at fifteen, Christianity seemed easy, accessible, and satisfied a spiritual dimension of my personality whilst not really challenging myself or anyone else. That sense lasted for about nine years until the abstract foundations, so flimsy to begin with, began to dissolve.

In 1990 I'd seen a documentary series on TV, *Through the Devil's Gateway: Women, Religion and Taboo*.[8] The episode I remember was about the rite of male circumcision as developed within the Hebrew male dominated culture and religion to be a means by which men could out-do the importance of female menstrual blood for the benefit of their increasingly patriarchal society and culture. For one thing, this incidence of women speaking about subjects hitherto deemed the exclusive province of male authority was a real shock to my twenty-four-year-old self at that time. I'd heard of goddesses through my long fascination with mythology but had been an Anglican Christian both in family culture and personally, as mentioned, from age fifteen.

In 1991 I travelled overseas, intent on searching the lands of my ancestors for clues to my identity, searching for personal meaning, and desperate to find my own voice. Then, back in Australia and while I was pregnant in 1992-1993, I heard Spider Redgold (The GoodWitch of Oz)[9] on the car radio, the subject witchcraft! I knew nothing about witchcraft, but it sparked resonant shivers in my

8   Alison Joseph, ed., 1990. *Through the Devil's Gateway: Women, Religion and Taboo*. A Channel Four Book, London, SPCK.

9   *Return to Mago* e*magazine <https://www.magoism.net/2016/04/meet-mago-volunteer-spider-redgold/>

body. Following the cardiac surgery for my son I moved with my husband to be closer to his workplace, and in a beautiful coincidence found myself living within walking distance of a lesbian and women-centred bookshop by the sea. Here I found books that were truly keys to unlock portals to consciousness: *The Serpent and the Goddess* (Mary Condren); *Casting the Circle* (Diane Stein); *The Myth of the Goddess* (Anne Baring and Jules Cashford); *Reweaving the World: The Emergence of Ecofeminism* (Irene Diamond and Gloria Feman Orenstein); *The Chalice and the Blade* (Riane Eisler). Seemingly random threads in an ordinary life. When they met in a deep place within me during and following the birth of my son, a profound paradigm shift took place. Goddess was the supernova, the shape of the new creation, and the song. I could take my dismembered self to Her; I could trust that I was not going to be berated or shamed as She and I worked to put me back together.

And so, it had been the birth of my first child and the precarious state I lived in for the five months following (until he had successful cardiac surgery) which enabled me to make the connections between my female body, the Judeo-Christian tradition, the wider society and the ideology underpinning it. It was overwhelming but I was fiercely determined to take the journey, to brave the unknown terrain of the paradigm shift. I kept a dream diary. I used the bibliographies of the first few feminist books I bought to track further female thought and vision, all the while learning to recognise patriarchy and the imperatives of domination all around me, and within myself. I began to allow myself to think about the traumas I'd experienced in my relationships with my parents, with men in my life, with other women, and the ongoing trauma of all life under patriarchy. I continued to do this most basic practise very much in isolation, gradually connecting with other women. Over the years I've tried to share Goddess with those who seek Her and that in itself has been a hard road: opportunity or lack thereof; so many women traumatised, the bloody birth work of the journey to Goddess – a going back and a going forth simultaneously – not always understood or Her value appreciated. Sometimes She's feared or frowned upon because the patriarchal mind wants to continually prioritise men.

And so it wasn't until several years had passed, and after the birth of my daughter and the end of my marriage that I came to realise how Goddess Feminism and the Women's Spirituality movement had introduced me to a form for holding and shaping my understandings of life, a model for female authority, maternal giving values and power-with, the ability to respond to life creatively with ethics and integrity, a cohesive symbol for cosmic principles, and a means by which to navigate, and restore from trauma. I'd had none of those tools and creative connections from the dominant culture, and even finding solidarity with other women was far from easy. But in moving forward with Goddess as I found Her within and around myself, I never looked back. Goddess had connected me to multidimensional life, an energy and a participatory community of women throughout time, history, and prehistory. I had found Goddess did not insist life an illusion or the body less-than in some energy hierarchy which must be purified or transcended either physically or metaphysically. Goddess did not traumatise, but nor did she trivialise or suppress our terrible hurts.

Goddess is tangible ground, source, process, return. She is winged thought, vision, stories that make sense and do not insist on patriarchal contortions and reversals. The healing bloom I have found sits at the crossroads of the cosmic, the terrestrial, the social, and the woman I am always becoming. As a writer and artist, I can vision forward through a Goddess imaginary. When my heart bursts open, I can weave songs of blood and love. I can share plans of discovery, allow my tongue to try new shapes of language, and sketch maps to potential affiliation with others. I can participate in life re-membered.

Withstanding the Storm

Arlene Bailey

I'm a walking mess right now because
my beloved of 50 years is dying
If ever there was time for brutal, raw
honesty this is it but sadly, I am told
I must be brave and hold all I feel at bay

Don't let him see you cry!
Don't let him hear your nighttime keening!
Don't let him know you wear your
broken heart on your sleeve!

Keep a stiff upper lip, raise your chin,
smile so he doesn't see the mess you are

Brush your hair and put on your
best face so he will know you care,
so he won't see, in Your face,
His shrinking body and gaunt features

Pretend!
Hide!
Pretend!
Hide!

Wear the mask
Wear the mask
Wear. The. Effing. Mask!!!

I hear myself scream as I once again
tell Patriarchy to STFU and quit telling
me how I, as a woman, need to be,
act, look, feel in every single situation,
on and on ad nauseum

I will not diminish my emotions,
nor hide the despair of the woman
who is this walking mess

I will not...

Oh My Goddess, don't say it! Stop!
Don't label yourself as traumatized!

NO! I will not stop...

I will not pretty up my face so he
doesn't know I've been crying,
nor hide my fears and innermost
thoughts in the guise of protecting
him from what He already sees,
what He already knows within!

I will be seen in all the messiness
that comes from the loss of a
lifetime of memories now fading
in the body of the one I love

I will be seen in my heartbreak,
my anguish and, yes, even fear

For you see...

While others try to force onto me
their uncomfortable feelings around
the process of death...

Force onto me the idea that I need to
hide the mess that is Me, rather than
the idea of embracing all my emotions...

Tell me I must be brave because
I am the lucky one...

The lucky one? Really?

While everyone tries to bleach white
this very messy process of dying and
being with the dying, this messy business
of trauma and the traumatized...

I have a secret they do not know
A secret Goddess whispered to me
one night as she held me in the depths
of my anguish and heartbreak

A secret only those in deep trauma
can see, touch, feel, transform

A secret that she wrapped me in as
She dried my tears and strengthened
my knowing that SHE is always here
holding me, hearing my rants and
screams as I melt into the nothingness
of the abyss of one so deeply traumatized

The secret?

My emotions,
Any and all of them,
Are
My
Superpowers!

And

When I can stand in the fullness of
all the chaotic energies flowing
through and around me...

Stand without succumbing to the
all-encompassing nature of grief...

Stand without caving in, but rather
allowing the woman I am to be held
in the belly of the Creature I am...

Stand while being held in the soft
embrace of the Great Mother and my
Council of Goddesses, while calling
in my Ancestors and cloaking it all in the
depths of ancient, transformative, ritual...

When I can walk into the Lake of Avalon,
stand in her ancient primordial waters and
not succumb to the depths as I reclaim my
Sword of Personal Sovereignty and Empowerment,
knowing Goddess does not live outside of me,
but rather IS me...

Then and only then am I able to shift
the trauma that holds me hostage
to less than my empowered self

Then and only then am I able to
withstand the storm that is this now

Going In

Arna Baartz

Becoming the Breath Between

Arlene Bailey

For the past three years I have been in transition. Some would say a journey of discovery. It has been both and... it has been death, suffering, illusion, awareness, descent (somewhat different than death, though a prelude to such), ascent, going in circles, standing still, lost in the dark, peaking at a hint of light, bathing in lots of light, finding me, losing me, meeting new me, drowning, surfacing, spiraling... spiraling... spiraling.

~We are told in the face of adversity we are to continue to smile and stay in a place of love.

~We are told to embrace change, even (especially??) if that change comes as the crashing Tower of the Tarot destroying everything. After all nothing is permanent.

~We are told that when death (metaphorical/symbolic) comes calling we are to deepen into ALL our feelings, acknowledging them and letting them surface.

~We are told don't attach.

~We are told to name the negative and release it.

~We are told don't focus on the negative; all will be well if we just focus on the positive.

~We are told to allow and name the fear rather than burying it.

~We are told don't acknowledge fear.

~We are told don't struggle.

~We are told anything worth having is worth fighting/struggling for.

~We are told change is good and that deep transitions create our medicine, our sacred work.

Whew! So many things we are told. So many impossible contradictions. So many voices telling us what is best. Many times – usually – from voices that have not the same experience(s), we are told, whatever we do, do not take on the label of trauma!

Although I already knew this from a point of insight, I have come to feel it in my bones. Change comes to us whether we want it or not, whether we are ready or not. Life is not static. Sometimes the change that comes is on the surface another's change, but if we are in relationship, we are affected too... differently perhaps, but just as deeply and profoundly. Regardless, it is change and it happens, and it is a maze with no instructions that we now must navigate. It may be a symbolic death, but at times it feels very real. At times we may even want it to be real.

For the longest time, I struggled with the incongruousness that lived in all the advice, all the wisdom shared by teachers, friends, family, new age wisdom, ancient mystery teachings.

How was I supposed to acknowledge and accept while also focusing on only one side of the continuum? The questions haunted me. If I acknowledge only the light, only love, giving no voice to fear or darkness where does that leave me? Conversely, if I deepen into the shadow, the negative, the suffering, how am I ever to come up for air, for life?

For the longest time after the earthquake that started this roller coaster, I felt like I was simply in the void. Not the void of creation – on the edge or event horizon – smack dab in the middle of the darkest of the darkest, the deepest of the deep. I raged and raged and felt like Inanna on the meat hook stripped of everything I knew, everything I believed, everything I had worked for and held dear, everything that identified me as me. Unlike Inanna, however, I didn't go willingly into this place nor was I interested in any understanding. I just wanted my life back, the way I thought my life should look like, the way this stage of my life (my Crone years) should be. Each time I felt like I could ascend and grasp onto some semblance of normalcy, the dark sister, Erishkigal, yanked me back and the darkness once again swallowed me. You didn't come willingly, you haven't learned, you don't understand, you're not ready, she hauntingly said.

I'm not sure when things began to shift or what changed. These last three years contained moments of vast darkness and moments of incredibly beautiful love-filled experiences of lightness of being. Shadow work, dreams, psychotherapy, shamanic journeying, Shamanic Breathwork, visions and more visions, new found psychic abilities, new found and reclaimed abilities in art and writing, ancestral and past life memories, messages from the oldest of the oldest Goddesses, messages from Angels, messages from feline familiars on this plane and beyond the Veil, messages and mystery teachings from beloved teachers along with LOTS of solitude and walks in the woods and ritual, ritual, ritual... THANK GODDESS FOR RITUAL... all parts of the puzzle of putting me back together or rather birthing a new me. Accepting that I was in the depths of trauma and my only way out was going in and allowing Her to remake this being that is me.

One day recently I had another of my light-bulb-turning-on epiphanies...

Life is paradox. OK, that's not such an epiphany, but it was the beginning. The ah-ha moment came when I realized that it is by stepping into the paradox and allowing it to wrap around us like a cloak, that the mask comes off and our eyes actually open. It's not about just understanding or acknowledging the paradox, we must become the paradox. In my case, the paradox was named trauma and there wasn't just one layer, but multiple layers and hence multiple paradoxes that would demand to be seen and heard and experienced.

One has to allow the darkness, one has to allow the suffering, the descent, freely and loudly acknowledging the pain, the distress, the disappointment, the illusion AND one has to do this through the love of the light and the dark. There must be both sides... two seemingly incongruous possibilities, i.e., the paradox...or there is no homeostasis, no balance. Further, if we only allow one side, we risk being lost in the illusion of what is real, what is not real, and even more importantly what can be real.

It's not about one side or the other, not about only light, or only dark, but about both. Not only about how we think things exist or should exist, but the potential for how they can exist. This is how Mother Nature is, how Goddess is. She does not have only one side. She does not deny dark in favor of light or vice versa. She does not permit life without death nor death without life. She is both of these and all of this and everything in between and while there are times that one is stronger than the other, both sides... light and dark... birth and death... are necessary for wholeness, for completeness, for the homeostatic integrity of the system.

It was only after I realized I had to allow for the both/and, that I had to approach everything through my heart... through love... that I had to tap even deeper into my connection with Goddess and her cycles and ways of being and knowing and living...that I had to allow for the incongruousness of it all... that things began to shift and the light began to grow stronger. It was only after all of this that I understood the need for the darkness, for the metaphorical death that I could once again begin to embrace life.

By acknowledging the dark, the so-called negative... by giving voice to our fears, our disappointment, our shadow, our trauma, we break the hold these things have on us, and we are no longer attached. By allowing the juiciness of the dark, we are actually able to see and embrace the light. In contrast, if we simply bury the dark, the negative, our light is dimmed and there is never true balance, true wholeness. If we deny paradox, we deny potential. If we don't allow for the seemingly incongruous, we can't achieve homeostasis and that place of internal stability, that place of internal strength.

Going one step further with the idea of becoming paradox... It is not enough to just become the paradox of both light and dark. Actually, we must become the breath between – neither light nor dark, but both super imposed into a seemingly single existence, existing in a place of simply being present. Only then are we not at odds with the seemingly incongruous.

I'm not sure when this shift happened, when Goddess removed enough of trauma's tendrils, but I knew I'd lived in the dark long enough, done my work there, and now it was time to return to the surface. I could finally break free from Erishkigal's grip.

So where am I presently? Hmmm... still not sure. I do feel movement, but I also know that I am still in the void, still in the cauldron of rebirth and regeneration, not completely ready to spring forth... not just yet.

However...

I am swimming closer to the edge, now able to touch the proverbial rim of the event horizon – that place of unfathomable possibility and birth. Although I'm not sure what comes next, I am OK with that. It is enough to finally feel and know I am moving from process to being. It is enough to simply exist in the present knowing I have been marked by the Infinite.

I am living from my heart, illusions of what should be gone, more accepting of what is, understanding nothing is permanent, understanding that when others said my darkness – my trauma – made them uncomfortable it was not about me, understanding and accepting that both light and dark may exist in the same day, the same moment and, all in all, ready for whatever comes next.

Interestingly, in keeping with Her ways, all of this realization and movement has occurred since Imbolc. I am coming out of the dark, feeling desire stirring, just as She begins to move. The Old One is speaking, but it is the Maiden I feel and see.

Goddess continues to walk beside me.

And So It Is.

Author's Note:

I wrote the original of the above in 2017 while deep in the transformative depths of a Scorpio transit at the same degree of my Sun and Chiron and a life altering experience around the loss of my partner's job right before retirement. I now know this was trauma*, though at the time I did not have that language or understanding, and I struggled to understand what was happening much less how to shift it. Truly, I thought I was dying, wanted to die and, if not for some major intervention from what and who I call Goddess, I probably would have ended my life.

Fast forward to 2021 and, once again, I find myself mired in these depths, though this time from my partner's imminent dying. Trauma has come for a visit settling in with that smirk and a torch, laying waste to all I've known or am. Thank Goddess I have a greater understanding of how insidious trauma and sister grief can be and how there are layers and layers covered in tendrils that can trap one in a great untethering and unraveling. If not for Goddess,

She in her myriad of forms and visages... if not for Her and all the ways She holds me and sustains, teaches and transforms me, I would be lost and helpless.

This time though my medicine basket is full of new experiences from the past years. Plus, I have greater and deeper wisdom and access to the medicine of my own tools in addition to Her's. While I still have deep relationship with Inanna and Erishkigal, I now also walk with some powerful badass women in the guise of the Goddesses An' Morrighan, Lilith, Medusa, and Isis and the real-world Goddess, Queen Boudicca of the Iceni whose sword allows me to cut through a lot of the bullshit that comes labeled as help. Further, I now have the deeply transformative tools of paint brush and pen and wield them like a sword from a place of deeply empowered understanding, sovereignty, and acceptance.

Perhaps, most importantly, I recognize trauma for what it is AND how it can be an ally if we allow the process of grief and our own dying to become the dark matter thrust into the fires of the alchemist... if we allow ourselves to become gold. If we can name trauma and willingly submit to the depths where Hecate as Grandmother teaches us the inner dark mysteries, submit to Erishkigal and symbolic death and allow, allow, allow... never chastising ourselves for where we are or what we cannot do... if we can walk with Goddess on the Camino that is the path of trauma, taking each day as it comes and trusting She has a plan, we can become a stronger and more deeply transformed being with an ending that comes cloaked as a new beginning.

Does all of this make trauma a welcome guest or an easy one? Oh Hel No! Fuck that shit!

However... With the allies of Goddess and Ritual, Art, and Writing, I was able to create an opening for not just surviving trauma but eventually transforming it into something truly life changing. At least that was my experience throughout 2017 and now once again as I move through these last months of 2021. At the writing of this, I'm still in process so I guess we shall see how it all lands.

*Slight additions and reworking of 2017 original writing to add the word trauma.

Shapeshifting Trauma

Arlene Bailey

The wolf stalks me in my dreams
She comes in my waking hours too
holding me in her wild ways as trauma
threatens to silence me, drowning me
in the insidiousness of the impossible

I feel her cold nose as she tries to wake me,
tries to rouse me from that place of frozen
fear and tears that threaten to drown me

She cries in the night, she cries in the day
howling for me to follow her across unknown
landscapes and into the forbidden depths
where trauma lives, where it waits

Her howling awakens my soul with a
hunger for her wildness, her holy way of
focusing on the present, no knowledge or
desire for what has been nor what is to come,
only what is present in the now

She does not allow her mind to replay over
and over the events that brought trauma,
but rather sits beside me holding a space
for the ineffable to be felt and the insidious
to be silenced, holding a space where I feel
safe and sacred and able to choose my healing

As I close my eyes and open my mind it is not
Wolf I see, but a woman holding the radiance of a
thousand candles with flames as bright as the sun

Wolf is a woman with no signs of age and
simultaneously all ages and stages of life,
marked with the scars of one who has faced
the battering and bruising from her demons
just to name that which holds her hostage

Wolf comes as Goddess in the night
in a Shapeshifting ritual of transformation
and empowerment as the cloak of trauma
drops from the woman's very being

Silencing the voices that held her hostage,
Wolf who became Goddess who becomes
Woman now stands in authentic being
knowing she is both holy and whole

Vision Weaver
Arlene Bailey

©Arlene Bailey

When I Met the Goddess

Helena Anderson

When I met the Goddess, I was already cut open. Already poisoned and I oozed. On the rare occasion I touched, I touched from need, I touched to control. I touched and I infected others.

When I met the Goddess, I gave nothing that did not benefit me, center me, profit. I was an agent, a rebel, a man inside a girl. Always fighting, always right-ing. I was abused and I abused others.

When I met the Goddess, I was bargaining. I would never bargain with God. I would subdue him. I knew him. He had nothing I wanted. He was for the weak.

When I met the Goddess, I was looking up and breathing deep. I was scared. Maybe for the first time in my life. My — 'hit me again, I can take it.' 'I can drink any man under the table,' 'don't touch me, don't you want me,' 'look what I will do.' you can't have me' — life was a numb life, a meaningless life.

For this moment, I was suspended, new in unknown territory because deep inside my sabotaged self, a gift had come to me and for the first time I had something to lose. A child.

When I met the Goddess, I was ragged and diseased but for the first time I wanted to be in service. I wanted to care about something, I wanted to mean something.

When I met the Goddess, I breathed, and I promised her my life if She would teach me how to live long enough to see my son marry. I promised her my life if She could teach me to feel, if She could show me a life worth living. And so, she showed me the blue of the sky, the green of the plant, and She asked me why I liked so much my songs of pain.

When I met the Goddess, her word was connection and it made me sick. Good she said. Throw up all that man-made food. Your Mother will feed you now. I was afraid and I did not trust her and she did not abandon me. I said no and she said I love you anyway. She knew I did not know how to trust. She knew how to be kind. The Goddess taught me patience.

When the Goddess and I had forged a two-year friendship. I was sick but still strong. I was fighting an illness with machines and chemicals, money and strength. I had become accustomed to needles and cuts. I drank radiation and aborted a baby. My body was a war. I was fighting. I was strong and I could take it and I was dying and...

When the Goddess and I had forged a two-year friendship, it occurred to me for the first time to ask her about her story. My dream she said. 400 million years. I was born and I had no language. I lived in joy and pain. I ate. I died. I birthed. I killed. I multiplied and diversified. I reveled in creating as many different versions of myself as I could imagine. Then one day I learned to speak—and in the beginning, I spoke only of me. The whole me... I was a celebrity. I was named Goddess. But a part of me, my son, wanted to be God apart from me and I have to admit, I wanted to experience the world as him. Experiment with force. Rebel, dominate and be dominated. These were feelings I had not experienced. So, for an age I lost myself in power and learned all I could about it but now at the end I am tired, and I move into a New Age with new knowledge. Together I am healing as the Mother, healing as the Father, healing as the Friend, and now I call all the joyful, all the healing parts of me together and I put them first. And when I am done, we will be a family again. A better family than even we were before.

When the Goddess and I had forged a two-year friendship, I decided to get sober, to write a book, to raise my son, and to leave my country.

When I became the Goddess, I cried and laughed for the first time in years. I made a path to my peace, my healing. I stopped fighting. I stopped exercising. I gave up my stuff, my car, my running water. I went to live among my guides. I moved to the Matriarchy.

When I became the Goddess, I let go of the idea that I wasn't important enough, or that I should be dead. I claimed my right to relax. I learned to meditate and journal. I learned to love myself and accept myself. I faced my toxic patterns. I wanted to live, and I wanted to live good.

When I became the Goddess, I asked forgiveness from my Mother, my partner, my child, and myself. I dedicated myself to the privilege of connection. I let go of anger, worry, control. I de-centered, I gave up competition. I discovered the joy in the joy of others, and I started riding a bike.

When I became the Goddess, I healed myself. My whole self. My feminine, my masculine, and my child self. I gave myself what I wanted from others, and I became a woman. I shed my skin. I left the Patriarchy and I joined the new world. And I joined in the groups of the other women.

Solstice Moon in a Land of Strife

Barbara O'Meara

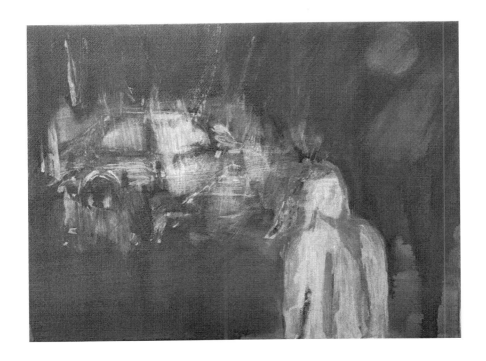

Normalizing Abuse and Exploitation = Trauma

Anonymous

I was teaching the Unitarian Universalist Cakes for the Queen of Heaven series, and a young woman came to me at a break. Tearfully, she said she regretted she had to leave. She believed in and supported the content of the course but to take it in, embrace it in her life, meant a total overhaul of her life. She knew her husband would fight her, as would her in-laws and her own family. She didn't want to lose her kids. It was easier to put it out of her mind and submit to the yoke under which she was living—or so she thought. Even incremental change seemed impossible. I often think of her and wonder where she is today. I also learned you can't un-ring the bell and unlearn what you've learned. Maybe she wasn't ready then to walk away, or take small steps to free herself, but I pray she found a way out.

Another example of questionable choices comes to mind when I read about a woman who knew her husband's male friend was being inappropriate with young women, even her daughter's friends. When confronted about whether she was going to speak to her husband about his friend, the woman angrily responded by saying, "Do you want me to give up my marriage and the privileges that come with it?"

So often, we women perpetuate the sins of abuse and exploitation because society has put women in marginalized situations where they have to rely on abusers or exploiters for their quality of life. Instead of teaching sons social justice at their knee, women often play it safe and teach patriarchal values to their sons and daughters, continuing the cycle of abuse. In my opinion, it's these abusers and their willing cohorts who are still today fighting against equality for women. They also don't want a woman to control her own reproductive health because that gives women more choices. It's easier to control someone who is economically strapped or trapped with the care of children. But these are the things that happen to other women. Not me, a savvy feminist, teaching women not to be abused by patriarchy. Or so I thought.

At my second Saturn return, around the age of sixty, a time when one often takes stock of life, I started thinking more about the past decades due to a tumultuous transition I was living through at the time. Like scenes from a movie, I saw in my mind's eye my mother being pushed down the steps and thrown out of the house by my stepfather who had been at the local bar. It became normal and a learned behavior. We would go over to my grandma's house and wait for things to cool down. I can remember my mother cajoling my father over the phone and soon we'd return home. I coped by throwing myself into my school work, rarely bringing anyone home because I didn't know what I might find. Dad might be really awesome, because often he was, or he might be in one of those darker or hurtful moods. My body image never recovered from comments he would make like "It must be jelly 'cause jam don't shake like that." Mom and my stepdad taught me the roller-coaster ride of domestic violence. The blow-up followed by the make-up, a pattern of abuse which followed me into my work life and what I endured from male bosses. I didn't know I should name that behavior I saw all too often as abuse. It was just marriage—or work.

My stepfather eventually left my mother. He told her he was going home to visit family in a faraway state. While he was there, he blindsided my mother by serving her with divorce papers. He left her, unemployed, with me and my ten-year-old stepsister to care for alone, and $300 in the bank. There was never enough money in those years. I can remember my mother in tears, pleading with the man at the bank for credit because her name was on the checks. For years she relied on my grandmother who helped with money from her janitorial job, an ordeal teaching me the fear of economic uncertainty. I learned I never wanted to be at the mercy of anyone economically again.

Living with my mother was hell. I realize now she was afraid, frustrated and felt deserted but I could only see she turned to cheap beer to numb herself. I just kept my nose to the grindstone and set my sights on graduation a few years away so I could escape. Going back to senior year in high school, I was surprisingly nominated for prom queen. I knew odds were not good I'd win but my esteem experienced a little boost at being nominated—until I saw the popular girls whispering and laughing at me as we gathered to have our pictures taken before the voting began. My first taste of the abuse meted out by mean girls. When I told my mother in a rare moment of sharing, she warned me not to trust other women. They were all jealous of each other and it was a dog-eat-dog competition for men.

I graduated early—third in my class of over 300 students. I quickly got a job before graduation, when most of my friends were still living the life of a teenager.

When I bought my own high school ring and graduation picture wearing my cap and gown, my mother was clearly jealous, as remarks revealed that she had never enjoyed the privilege of such a thing.

Instead, I heard about the derogatory nicknames her family had for her. There were no words of congratulation or pride for a daughter from her mother. On my first payday, my mother expected me to turn over my entire check to her, rather than her going back to work to support herself and my stepsister. That was the final straw after years of hiding in my room. She was often drunk and angry or screaming. She'd driven her car into the back of my boyfriend's car in one of her drunken rages. I hated my job at an insurance company, but that paycheck was my way out of the day-in and day-out misery I was living with my mother. Her demand that I stick around in this misery and financially support her triggered my first solo walk into the unknown, though today, I'm not proud of how I managed it.

I took a page out of my stepfather's book—and disappeared from my mother. She didn't know where I was for quite some time because I couldn't risk what she might do in a jealous or drunken rage. About a year later, I came out of hiding, and I shared with my family I planned to marry my part-Hispanic high school sweetheart, who I had dated for five years—for love and security. I never considered the many other options. No one encouraged me to see how much bigger the world was with all its many roads to travel—but now I realize, to my family, the world offered few options beyond this small view of life. No family members threw me a wedding shower.

Instead, I remember my mother—apparently jealous of the wedding dress I paid for with my meager earnings—and my new father-in-law, along with my new husband, who took credit with his family for the modest wedding reception I had paid for.

My husband and I were together about seven mostly happy years until I realized he was more like my brother. We never had children, fortunately, which was by choice, but I often wonder the effect my mother had on that life decision because of the times she'd comment in disgust and shame about the "brown-skinned babies" we might make together.

When I ran away and disappeared and began my own life anew, I thought I'd escaped unscathed and left all the misery and woe behind. But I've come to realize unless we get help, these experiences shape our decisions for years to come. My family trauma was probably not as bad as some. I was never molested. I had food on the table and roof over my head. Yet traumatic psychological occurrences follow us for most of our lives and leave their marks, sometimes benign, other times not so much. And during all of this, I did not know to call any of it abuse or trauma. It was the way life was. Nowhere was there anyone asking, "How is your quality of life?" No one asked about my dreams or encouraged me to have a dream. I got the idea living life was about inevitable struggle and suffering—just like Jesus on the cross at mass where I'd been forced to go for so many years every Sunday. Today I believe that symbol of Jesus sends an intentional message of suffering and sacrifice being normal and noble, thus conditioning us to submit and accept abuse and exploitation aka religious trauma.

Fast forward twenty years. Life threw me a real curve ball.

I was assaulted by a young woman with a gun. My work life was crashing in large part because of the post-traumatic stress that it brought on. Therapy was awakening the abuse I was finally seeing in my past and in my workplace. I was a lot like that woman of domestic violence riding the ups and downs of the roller coaster, trying to hang on, when she really needed to recognize the trauma and walk away. Then my husband fell and hit his head and suffered a brain injury. We lost our jobs, income and the roof over our heads and were forced into disability and early retirement in an isolated place far away. It is hard to recall everything we went through for several years and I've chosen to write this as Anonymous because some of it I'm not allowed to talk about by way of a non-disclosure agreement to keep me quiet.

Long story short, supported by good friends, the Goddesses Isis and Sekhmet, the values of sacred feminine liberation thealogy and Nature surrounding me, I began to heal. It took several years though. At first all the chaos of the change left me with deep anxiety. Where we lived the internet was spotty making reliable communication difficult. I literally would hear the floor boards creak and be terrified the foundations were falling out from under me. I'd dream the house walls were full of holes to the outside and there was no roof. The snow paralyzed me with fear after almost slipping off the mountain in my first attempt to drive. The isolation from friends and the familiar weighed on me and I was terribly lonely. I didn't yet see the gift She'd laid out for me, waiting for me to open my eyes and relax and breathe. But it happened... slowly, like a slow-dripping faucet that turns into a flowing spigot. Not only did our isolation keep us safe for the worst year of the Covid-19 pandemic, but soon Mother Nature began to work Her magic on me. I felt embraced in my little wooded valley with Mother Mountain to the north and south as if She were hugging me. The bees and butterflies danced just beyond our porch in the morning light. The rabbits ran across the yard, darting from bush to bush. The blue-jays, quail and red-headed woodpeckers came to feast most mornings from the feeder. I loved seeing their little footprints on newly fallen snow. I began to notice the turning of the seasons and the changing of the leaves.

I had time now for my right brain work. I was working Her magic. Reading. Writing. Healing. Reflecting. Friends who stuck with me, I saw as lionesses in my pride—Sekhmet Sisters. Times like these you really know who your friends are. I realized I was no longer that hamster on the wheel. I wasn't a slave to the 9 to 5 grind. I could stay up until 2am and sleep until noon if I felt like it. I had no deadlines. My only job was to heal and help my husband do the same. And we were doing it every day, slowly, in Her loving embrace which I felt not so much as the public activist anymore, but more as an actual microcosm of the macrocosm, a part of Her web of life, breathing everyday here on our mountain, inhaling and exhaling. I'd escaped the wasteland. The chaos and challenges it took to uproot us from the trauma we were living was the price we paid for this gift.

I like to look under rocks and explore new ideas, even reconsider what the status quo might disparage. I'm a firm believer we have to rethink everything, even if that upsets our personal emotional apple cart. We can't bury our heads in the sand. We have to look at change as a vehicle for personal transformation, because if we're not growing, we're stagnant. Every opportunity to walk away toward a healthier option, to create healthy boundaries, is a gift. It doesn't mean we have to go out tomorrow and turn life on its head, but we can begin to plot or contemplate a new course.

Fortunately, fear of change is getting easier to manage as the decades pass. Life is showing me that walking away, and transition or transformation is not a "once and you're done" thing. Like Isis shaking her sistrum so the energies of the universe don't become stagnant, I believe these changes in life are necessary for us to keep growing and evolving, transitioning, changing, overcoming—and seeing the gift in these challenges that shape who we are. I have and still do actively purge toxic relationships, associations and ideas from my life, or at least, as best as I can. Abuse and trauma are not welcome or normal in my life anymore. I am simply not willing to pay that price for anything anymore.

Red Saves Herself

Natalie Celine Couillard

Under the HOOD of the hushed "LITTLE woman"
a seething fever burns blood RED.
Her weary heart seeking a cure among a mass of living dead.
RIDING solo into battle on the darkest night
to find her way home, into the arms of her own light.
All the paths she's been led through so far
have only shown her where the cloaked wolves are.
The wolves
with the steely, lecherous eyes
their roaming gazes charged
with cunning grandiose lies.
The wolves
with the sin laden, slap schooling hands
that took control of her mind and body
under strict demands.
The wolves
with the sharp predator teeth and venomous bite
that left her with monstrous scars
clutching a poisonous fright.
So, as she braves the next long road
she carries with her that basket load,
and when she can no more bear its hefty weight
she drops their macho burdens and opens a gate.
The divine huntress comes, the wolves at stake
wide awake... she takes back her fate.

Lineage of Mothers

Katrina Stadler

7 Ways Mothers Perpetuate Patriarchal Trauma in Their Daughters

Dawn Perez

This is the story of a little girl.

She loved to sing, to dance, to create. She had a heart of gold, pure and happy, but she was a child and needed guidance.

When she made a mistake or said the wrong thing, her mother would shut her out and pretend she didn't exist for days on end.

When the girl sang, her brothers said, "Knock off that noise."

When she needed care and emotional support, her mother said, "If you don't go through this by yourself, you'll never learn," and turned her back to her.

As the girl got older, she embraced theater and wanted to go into communications in college. Her parents said, "No, you're going into nursing."

Communications was much too strong a field for a daughter of a blue-collar worker to pursue. Nursing meant caring for others—it was much more a fitting career choice for a woman who knew her place: in the background, never seeking attention or care for herself.

But still, her spirit continued. She played guitar for her niece. She sewed her own clothes.

That woman got married and had her own children. Crippled with anxiety after the birth of her son, she gave up many of her creative endeavors and took to caring for her children as her only outlet in her home life. She practiced self-care in pieces, bit by bit when she had a minute to herself.

In her forties, she made one last attempt at searching out what her soul needed. She went back to school and became a massage therapist and healer. But quickly, she developed Carpal Tunnel Syndrome and had to stop.

Life had beaten her down, time and time again. She had lived her life without the healing embrace of her mother to help guide her way. She was alone, without her creativity or spirit, and without her dreams.

That woman is my mother. Broken. Bitter.

It reminds me of the quote by Dr. Clarissa Pinkola Estés: "There is a time in our lives, usually in mid-life, when a woman has to make a decision – possibly the most important psychic decision of her future life – and that is, whether to be bitter or not. Women often come to this in their late thirties or early forties. They are at the point where they are full up to their ears with everything and they've "had it" and "the last straw has broken the camel's back" and they're "pissed off and pooped out." The dreams of their twenties may be lying in a crumple. There may be broken hearts, broken marriages, broken promises."

When I had a miscarriage and came to my mother, crying for support, she snapped, "What do you want me to tell you?"

And when I tried to talk to her about some taboo topics that were important to me and my values, she said, "You're just trying to emotionally manipulate me!"

And when I called her out on all the times she had withheld compassion from me as a child and young adult, she said, "If you had told me the severity of what was happening, I would have been more compassionate."

No. She wouldn't have.

I love my mother, and I know that she is a good person. But she couldn't have given me the help, support, or compassion I had needed because she had never *been shown* compassion as a child. She had never been given emotional support. She had never been taught to stand on her own two feet, empower herself, or even embrace other women.

And it was the same with her mother before her and *her* mother before her. Broken. Bitter.

When we think of the patriarchy, we think of white men. We think of those with power and money, making others submit to their will. We think of all their lies, deception, and violence against women and ethnicities they deem "lesser than."

But in my life, the most pervasive source of patriarchal trauma came from my own mother, as it has been with so many other women in this world.

We know the reasons that our mothers perpetuate the patriarchy. It's love—they are protecting their daughters (and sons) from that violence, teaching them to be small, fly beneath the radar and not become ostracized from society, or worse, killed.

But we *don't* always know how to recognize the trauma and how it shows up in our lives. We think of it as generational differences or psychological issues, but we rarely give it credit for what it really is: perpetuating patriarchal violence and trauma.

I personally saw patriarchal trauma from my mother show up in seven different ways in my life.

1) Judgment

When we witness our mothers judging other women, it is a violation of our feminine power. They might say things like, "She's too fat. She's too skinny. She needs to wear less makeup."

You've heard them all before. These judgments are meant to divide us. They help us see each other as competition instead of as sisters. Our judgments come directly from the patriarchy and our need to protect ourselves and always be guarded.

But this judgment also extends to themselves. When our mothers criticize themselves for their bellies jiggling, they are doing their daughters and sons a disservice in the name of the patriarchy.

2) Withholding Love

Patriarchal violence has made it so that women feel afraid to wholeheartedly embrace their children lovingly. To follow our instincts and pick them up when they cry. To kiss their ouchies and rock them to sleep.

We're told that rational thought and doing things themselves is better for our children (see #4). We're told that Cry-It-Out isn't harmful to them and that children can do things far before it's actually developmentally appropriate for them to do so.

This is so damaging to boys and girls alike, cutting children off from what should be their first and primary source of comfort in this world.

3) Shutting Down Creativity

Yes, denial of our dreams, creative lives, or spiritual selves is a form of trauma.

My mother was forced to become a nurse when she wanted to go into communications. While my parents gave me the freedom to choose whatever I wanted in college, I would have received backlash if I had chosen to become a lawyer, engineer, or doctor.

When we tell our daughters to stop singing, stop drawing, stop picking flowers, and stop dreaming, we force them to play within the patriarchy's rules. And we're doing the same to our sons when we push them into sports instead of allowing them to explore art.

Because no art is created within the patriarchy; all art and creativity directly oppose the forces that control our world. Defiance. Rebellion. And the white men that try to control us know this.

4) Forced independence

When children have love withheld from them, they're forced to be independent from a young age. We think of girls who take on responsibilities before they need to and then become "strong independent women" who don't need anyone later in life.

This is just another coping mechanism for being forced into a world where masculine ideals are praised, and feminine ones are spat upon.

Our true nature is to gather into communities, to be sisters, supportive of one another. But this is a threat to the patriarchy when women are stronger. We're no threat when we're "independent" and alone.

5) Shutting Down Questions or Curiosity

When a little girl asks questions and her mother shuts her down because it's uncomfortable or she doesn't know the answers, this is the patriarchy at work.

Women are naturally curious, but within the patriarchy, that instinct is dangerous, and thus it is shunned. Seeking a personal journey and looking for answers give a woman power.

But more than that, if a woman is asked a question and it makes her feel vulnerable, she shies away from it. The patriarchy teaches us that that vulnerability makes us weak, but the opposite is true.

6) Religion

Although my mother was never very religious, colonialist Christianity infested her life. She lived in "God's image," dedicating herself to others in selflessness. This became a source of evidence for her moral superiority to others who rejected upholding the patriarchal society.

"Taking the higher path" meant silencing her own voice for "the greater good" of mankind. She pushed aside her truth time and time again and taught me to do the same.

7) Energy and Words Not Being Aligned

This one often goes without being noticed. But our mothers who perpetuate the patriarchy know deep down that something is not aligned with themselves, which comes out in their energy.

And when they speak, it's on autopilot. Our mothers talk harshly in judgment, protecting evil men, victim-blaming, and "taking the higher path," and they have just a tinge of guilt beneath their words.

But when they withhold their own truths, you can hear the insecurity and pain in their voices. They say, "No worries, it's fine." But they mean, "I'm silencing myself even though you violated my boundaries."

Treating sons and daughters with passive aggression is trauma perpetuated by the patriarchy.

I have one more short story. It's the story of a boy whose father broke the line of patriarchal trauma in his own family. Of a boy who had compassion and love from his parents growing up. Who was encouraged to be creative. Who was witnessed for who he was and his own personal truth.

That boy grew up and became my husband. When the lines of patriarchal violence and trauma are broken, those individuals pass on the skills to help others break their generational trauma. Because he had the tools from his own father, he helped me break the cycles of trauma in my own ancestral line.

Now, my husband and I will raise our own children without the trauma that haunts my past, my mother's past, and his father's past.

Whenever I feel angry with my mother for siding with "The Man," victim-blaming or silencing my voice, I try to remember that she's just protecting herself, and she believes that she's protecting me.

But she is also severing herself from her innermost reservoir of truth, power, love, and joy.

We can do better. We *can* live in a way that heals that patriarchal trauma and taps into that fountain of the Goddess in all of us, for ourselves and for our children.

The Wisdom in Feeling Devoured
Edy Pickens Levin

The Wisdom in Feeling Devoured © Edy Pickens Levin 2021

The Wisdom in Feeling Devoured and Waxing Crescent Transmutation: How Goddess Helps Me with Trauma

Edy Pickens Levin

I've been working on "the shark painting," aka "The Wisdom In Feeling Devoured," for over a decade now. I crack its code at snail's pace, and every time I think I understand what it's teaching me, I fall off the painting wagon and spiral into another level of confusion. A halt in the painting process ensues. But I always come back. The image is currently both an unfinished oil painting as well as a Photoshop version of a future "finished" version of the original. I have intentions of going back into it as a part of my Samhain ritual this year. As usual, my piqued interest in revisiting the painting has coincided with a request by my employer to set up three goals for myself for this academic year. And, as usual, I am diving deeper than I can express in my annual Goal Meeting. Here's an attempt:

> "The ability to lie, to oneself and to others, is prominent in postconquest consciousness... People indoctrinated into the post conquest mindset are even more susceptible to deceit because they're conditioned to downplay sensory, emotional, behavioral, and intuitive input in order to focus on what someone is saying." —From *The Tao of Equus* by Linda Kohanov.

I read this over and over again. Then, I looked up "post conquest consciousness" because I was not familiar with it as a phrase, but I am so familiar with it and its powerful effect on my stress levels and my lived experiences.

I found this wonderful article by Christian de Quincy called Consciousness and Conquest.[10] Here are some words that really got my attention:

> In its search for truth, reason operates via conquistadorial dialectic: One idea, or one person's "truth," is confronted and overcome by an opposite idea or someone else's "truth." The clash or struggle between them produces the new synthesis—perceived as a creative advance in knowledge.
>
> By contrast, liminal or preconquest consciousness, in striving for what feels right for the collective, seeks to accommodate differences. When confronted by reason, it naturally wants to please the other, and so invariably yields. Reason strives to conquer, feeling strives to please, and the result: obliteration or suppression of liminal consciousness by reason.
>
> Even more disturbing to me was the realization that none of this implies malicious intent on the part of reason. Simply encountering an epistemology of feeling, reason will automatically overshadow it—even if its intent is honorable.
>
> As I looked back on my own career, I found plenty of confirming instances. In my work, I have had many occasions to engage people interested in consciousness from perspectives other than philosophy or science— mysticism, shamanism, aesthetics, for example. More often than not—even if I was trying to be considerate of their different ways of knowing—these people left the encounter feeling abused or squashed by having to match accounts of their experiences against the rigorous logic of rational analysis. When a search for truth pits dialectic

10 http://maaber.50megs.com/sixth_issue/epistemology_2e.htm

reason against dialogic experience the feeling component of the other's knowledge can rarely withstand the encounter. Feeling feels invalidated. Wisdom is blocked by "truth."

I read that and every panic attack and traumatic experience I've had became understood in a new way. My whole way of being is rooted in the pre conquest consciousness and is therefore, subject to being prey both in my patterned behavior as well as in our societal conditioning (which ultimately wrote my operating manual and which I am tearing out pages and currently rewriting.) The wisdom that I sense is available to me in every moment, is also the devoured. No wonder I have spent so much time feeling the jaws clamp down on me... and then being told that I'm the crazy one. My superpower is in being prey. My peaceful rose is inside the jaws of the shark. Being prey and not judging it or slipping into shadow victim patterns can be (if I surrender and let it) my source of wisdom. It is what this shark painting is leading me to uncover...

Leaning into the mouth of a shark and finding a sensual rose as my Soul's sensation is akin to choosing the belonging to myself and the wisdom I contain as truth over the pre-scripted belief that I am rotten to the core or on the wrong track. I just have to be willing to sit with the Shadow Self and practice that over and over until my wholeness is accepted. By Me. It is the opposite of seeking external validation.

My intention is to practice wholeness by sitting with what I am always trying to flee—the projections of others, my deep-rooted belief that I am unworthy, that I am eternally wrong, that I don't belong. It's following the wisdom that Toko-pa Turner sets forth in her book, *Belonging: Remembering Ourselves Home.* She says,

> "There's a big difference between staying positive and being generative. The first disregards hard truths, the second is the fruit of having composted them."

The shark painting is my artifact—the one I produce during my composting. It's the hardest truth.

In continuing to be curious about how I overcome trauma with Goddess help, I submit my painting, "Waxing Crescent Transmutation." This artwork is a watercolor that is also part of a series of mandala prints that are a visual representation of my physical and spiritual journey, a journey that has drawn on Goddess to help me every step of the way. I start by making intuitive paintings with free application of water media. Then, I digitize the abstract watercolors and further alter shapes with software that allows me to experiment with radial symmetry, light filters, and more. After this digital composition phase, I once again return to hand painting by transferring the image to watercolor paper and painting the digitally composed piece. The entire process is extremely self-referential and meditative in nature. It is metaphorically symbolic in its cyclical arrival into a yin or Goddess consciousness/container.

Each mandala is a tangible artifact from my journey—a special art piece that invites the viewer to enjoy the therapeutic benefits of the unique expressions that I bring to this world.

My process allows me to lean into the metaphorical symbolism of the Divine Feminine or Goddess. What I mean by this is that I participate in a painting ritual that aligns itself with the allowing and receiving of the cast-out underbelly of our human nature. That which has been cast as "weak" is actually wholeness—it is the unknown and the wild aspects of the human illusion we call life. Goddess guides me to release the patriarchal lens that informs the definition of "overcome" and this place of release is where I am finding myself as I ask for help from Goddess. Goddess supports trauma resolution by helping me remember that my body holds wisdom rather than blame, shame, and guilt as I have been taught by our patriarchal culture. With symbolic mark making that arrives with intuition and within this cyclical process. I reference and acknowledge the womb-like container that is a body inside an energetic field. I am grounded in my personal experience and remind myself that I can choose to sink into the body's wisdom as it shakes, pulsates, undulates, and ultimately guides me to allow my breath and movements to exist and be revered. I look for opportunities to allow my body's sensations to give me crucial information on how to support and care for myself, which naturally leads to a presence that becomes universal love. Patriarchy perpetuates trauma in the way that it also has the potential to bring me back to Goddess and thus, Oneness.

When patriarchy reinforces my separation from the body, Goddess continually offers me a container. Patriarchy seems to destroy and deny that container, but like a series of nesting dolls, it only finds that it is contained by (or contains) something larger (or smaller) than itself once again. My adherence to Goddess as guide helps me receive and expand within my container. Goddess teaches authentically while patriarchy deludes intentionally. My human mission and purpose is to remember the true teacher and wake up from the delusion. I can author a way of being that is aligned with Goddess as healer in the spaces where I have assumed false dominance—dissolve that delusion—listen and receive the support that is already there instead of striving to individually contrive a system built on false narratives. In this way, I find wisdom in the feeling of being devoured. This is a powerful tool in healing or "overcoming" trauma.

Waxing Crescent Transmutation

Edy Pickens Levin

Waxing Crescent Transmutation © Edy Pickens Levin 2019

Do You Know Her

C. Abigail Pingree

Do you know her? Have you seen her?

See, look... her picture.

See her all dressed up in childhood, an innocent light shining in her eyes. See her full pink cheeks and observe her smile.

She smiles because she knows she should. But she wants to rage and scream and tear out her broken heart. Do you see her? She is beautiful. She is brave, so brave.

Her courage and power have never been contained. And oh, how they tried. They could not force, beat and shame it out of her. They could not steal it away in the dark of night with pain and confusion. She stands still, all dressed up in childhood, an innocent light shining in her eyes.

Observe the quality of her stance and the clarity of her gaze. Her eyes gleam and hint at something compelling and formidable, something timeless and pure.

Do you know her? Have you seen her?

She has become lost, misplaced, gone missing; discarded for adult responsibilities and grown-up sensibilities. She wanders in solitude and in darkness, alone and afraid.

She is confused, she is troubled, and she is burdened. She is turned-round, dizzy, and bemused. She needs you to find her and to hear her. She has much to tell you:

> *"Don't turn away from me... feel my rage... hear my screams... speak to me of understanding."*

Look for her until you find her, for in her restoration your liberation lies.

The trees know her, the sky and the clouds too. The green springtime grass can tell you where she has gone, for her bare footsteps are remembered by the meadows and the pastures. The sun glistens with the same purity as the light that shines in her eyes, and the wind echoes with the delight of her laughter.

In stillness and quiet, every breath whispers her name. Listen. Her mother could not find her, her father could not either. But you can. You can find her if you look. She needs you to be bold. She needs you to be brave. What feels like defeat and dread may, in fact, be a longed-for reunion. An ached-for return to a place of peace and rest, of comfort and safety.

Do you know her? Have you seen her?

She longs simply to be taken up into loving arms, to know she is cherished and wanted, to be held close and never let go.

Tend to her sadness, heartbreak and pain. Watch over her well, with allowing and acceptance. Do not bid her go at your discomfort but welcome her to stay until, in exactly the right moment, she loosens her own tethers and sets herself free to soar and sing.

Do you know her? Have you seen her?

Find her. Let her innocent light shine once again and discover her true smile. Ease her pain and bring her home.

She needs you.

This is for her.

Heal
Megan Welti

COLLAPSE, MOTHER
Dawn Perez

All your life,
you've been told to hold it in.

Hold in your gut, woman,
Don't let them think you're fat.

Hold in your feelings, mother,
Don't let them think you're hysterical.

Hold in your worry, dear,
Don't let them think you're psychotic.

Hold in your grief, mama,
Don't let them see the pain in your heart.

Hold in your rage, woman,
Don't let them think you're unrefined, wild, feral, magick.

When you hold it all inside you,
Do you feel empowered?
Or do you feel exhausted?

You don't have to hold it in any longer, child,
I'm here.
You're safe.

Give it up.
Let it out.
Release it.
Let it go.

Collapse, mother.
Cry your tears and let them
Permeate the earth with their healing power.

You gut,
Your feelings,
Your worry,
Your grief,
Your rage.

It's all love, mother.
It's a part of you.

Embrace it, allow it.
Breathe it in.
Let it go.

Revolutions of Defiant Ecstasy:
Stealing Kali and Goddess Wisdom from the
Primordial Wave of Feminism

Claire Dorey

We can harness Kali's primal wisdom as a 'twelve step' map to heal from patriarchal wounding.

Reach out and you will find the Goddess. Run your fingertips through her history.

"Sorry Dharmic texts, I'm stealing Kali for a while. I'm stealing her so I can interpret her iconography in a way that is personal to me, because I think she can ease the path of suffering. I'm stealing her because I see her as an intergalactic vessel for processing the emotions of trauma when they are trapped in the body."

Kali belongs to the primordial wave of feminism. She is a revolutionary Goddess, and her wisdom is liberating. Her message transcends time and boundaries. As a symbol of female resistance, Kali is karma; a destroyer of evil and protector of the innocent; a champion for the survivors of patriarchy.

"To heal is to be empowered!" She says.
She wants us to stop blaming ourselves.

"Throw your trauma into the cosmic void and retrieve your intuition and innate creative wisdom." She says.

Kali is a tantric Goddess. There are many meanings for 'tantra', in Sanskrit, including: interweaving stories; spinning narrative; creating frameworks for practice and theory; happiness; expansion and spells – magic ingredients for the alchemy of transformative medicine. Tantra speaks to us as individuals, and we can interpret these abundant meanings in ways that are personal to us. Just like the universe, it is an expansive language, based on spiritual concepts and process. Sanskrit opens the mind. By engaging these principles, healing trauma becomes an esoteric journey!

Kali is a girl's girl — a fire eater, who has chosen to walk barefoot along the path of freedom. She's the festival girl you admire, a fire dancer, twirling her blazing baton, beneath the stars. Now you see her, now you don't, flames swooshing, music pulsing, back to dark. Arms spinning, gyrating hips, fleetingly illuminated by a corolla of flames, 'revolutions' of defiance and ecstasy, as the Milky Way passes overhead. Then back to black! Kali's Eternal Dance, represented by a skirt of many arms, is energy in motion.

1) 'Flow' Heals

Just as the Earth spins on Her axis, Kali's Eternal Dance is in constant motion. Movement shifts blocked emotion. Close your eyes and sway to the healing rhythm of the universe. Seek your ecstatic frequency in the primordial Shakti, the divine female energy, where the inconceivably violent forces of creation reside. Kali is never still. She is destroyer and creator; apocalypse and genesis; decay and birth; blood bath and incubator. Her medicine is deeply rooted in the cosmic cycles of death, birth, rebirth. Every woman holds patriarchal trauma somewhere in her body, so Kali urges us to let go, have fun, move our bodies, shake our hips and feel sensation. Undulate, jiggle, twerk, do restorative yoga. Find 'flow' to raise vibration and thaw emotion. Emotion in motion!

2) Move At Your Own Pace

The name Kali is derived from the Sanskrit word Kal which means time — the brooding womb of time. The Great Mother Creator of Time, says, "time heals!"

"Slow down, live life at your own pace, sit quietly, meditate and clear the space to honour your emotions."

3) Rummage In The Shadow

Just like the sky, poised to send storms and sunshine, Kali wears many shades. Day and night. Light and dark. Shadow and luminance. Blackness and radiance. Murk and clarity. As Kali Mata, the Dark Mother, she is brooding black and stormy blue. She is nirguna – the amorphic, transcendent void, where wisdom and safety lie. As Dakshinakali, the Protector Goddess, she is the wispy shade of a summer sky, where sunshine nourishes, and birds soar free. Blue sky thinking happens here.

The Dark Mother, who lingers in the cremation grounds and inhabits the liminal realms, tell us to blow the ash off, dig about in the graveyard and go face to face with the ancestors. When we learn our story, we discover we have a powerful lineage of female ancestors, stretching back to the womb of time. Empowerment is reaching back through time, to 'touch' the Goddess.

The key to healing is awareness, connection and release. Trauma manifests in many ways: disconnect, freeze, sadness, rage, depression, fear, anxiety, overwhelm, in action, running away, addiction, and self-sabotage. Kali says these emotions will eventually trap us into a corner. To run is to live in survival mode. Her message is clear, "You cannot escape your darkest fears, especially death, so drag your fears out of the shadow, look them in the eye, face them head-on and you will feel better for it."

It is not only the dark stuff that hides in the shadows. There's gold to be found. Rummage about and dig up the forgotten joys and the emotions you hid from the world. Trauma AND talent are hidden in the shadow. Both need to be dusted off.

4) Dare To Ask The Goddess For Help

There is power in the spoken word and in the manifestation of sound. Mantra is sound medicine for the soul. Kali is the sound of the universe, AUM (Om), the essence of everything and Her sound travels across the cosmic void on galactic strings. Chanting mantra has positive physiological and psychological effects, so send your vibration into the universe, where the laws of abundance reside. "Om Klim Kalika-Yei Namaha" is a Kali mantra recited to bring relief from thorny issues. Potent mantras, in micro-doses, set up positive vibrations in mind, body and cosmos.

5) Combat Patriarchal Silencing with Breathwork AND Yelling!

We need to talk about Kali's flame red tongue. Is it really about shame, apologies and gorging on blood? Or is this the tongue of a fire dancer, purging with flames, healing wounds? It seems clear to me that Her tongue directs us to talking therapy.

"Silence your inner critic AND exercise free speech!"
Her blood red tongue speaks with the yoni breath, connected to the blood root chakra, a direct conduit to Earth Mother – to a blood lineage of Goddess wisdom. Kali's cobra companion surges with kundalini, so flex the diaphragm, take deep breaths, and nourish the body with life force. Find your voice, speak unapologetically, beat your drum, scream, shout, sing, breathe!

Kali without Her Rajasic tongue is called Bhadra-Kali, the Decent-Kali, which illustrates patriarchal views on female compliance and shows how speaking out is not considered to be feminine! To which Kali replies, "......insert expletive!"

6) Sack Shame

Female trauma is communal trauma. It lies at the intersection of felt experience and perceived experience. It is violence and the threat of violence. It is clutching keys, walking home, at night.

Female trauma is communal shame. It is generational. It is a network of erased histories and legacies: plots to silence, control and subvert. Its most benign form is mansplaining. Its most destructive form is: rape; incest; trafficking; slavery; pornography; torture; witch hunts; domestic servitude; domestic violence; missing and disappeared women; religious bigotry; judgment; blame; hierarchy; environmental destruction; exploitation of Mother Nature; ownership; misogyny; fatism; ageism; racism; division; derision; pay gaps; poverty; FGM; child marriage; patriarchal domestication of the 'married womb' for breeding purposes; institutions that exploit and profit from unmarried mothers; miscarriage; paternal lines; being a mother; not being a mother; being labeled unclean – cursed; an array of knotted gynaecological symptoms; an array of cruel and imaginary scientific diagnosis, heaped on women, including hysteria, emotional irrationality and Stockholm syndrome.

Probably the most wounding cut of all: innocence lost to shame. "Close your legs," they ordered, "as we turned cartwheels in the sand. We we're feeling free and loving life! Then they body-shamed us with things we were too young to understand." Protect your daughters, "don't let them shame her!"

Grown up women, do cartwheels, spin hula hoops – 'revolutions' of joyful defiance and ecstasy!

7) Take Up Space

Kali's stance, in Goddess Pose, takes up space. Try it, it's harder than it looks! From the tips of her toes to the tips of her fingers this pose is about cosmic motion. Her hands are held in Mudra, ritual hand gestures, to direct energy within the body. One hand is poised in the Abhaya Mudra, to dispel fear.

The Kali Mudra, used in restorative yoga for healing anxiety and depression, is about pouring out and letting go. The mudra has interlocking fingers and closed thumbs, which, when twisted forward, open out into the yoni symbol – the symbol of the female generative power of the Shakti Goddess. Turn fear inside out!

8) Cut Through Illusion

Kali brandishes a sword and severed head, symbolising divine knowledge slicing through the ego, necessary for moksha – release from the karmic cycle of rebirth. Or is there more to it, such as cutting the crap, cutting what binds us, seeing with clarity?

By painting images of defiant women, brandishing severed male heads, female baroque painter Artemisia Gentileschi, alludes to the symbolic death of the rapist. She seeks revenge in paint, for future generations to witness, telling the aggressor, "You can escape but you cannot hide. Karma will catch up with you." Man's actions bow to greater forces – the karmic power of the Shakti Goddess and Mother Nature.

In the same way that Gentileschi paints patriarchal trauma, it seems to me that Kali Mata's iconography embodies what this looks and feels like. Creativity liberates, start doodling!!

9) Release Your Demons

The fifty-two skulls in the mundamala, the garland around Kali's neck, denotes Her as the Ultimate Reality. Perhaps the skulls also represent our attachment to our demons. One by one, in a measured approach, we can riffle our demons, like mala beads, and let them go.

10) Be Your Own Hero

The image of Kali standing on her consort Shiva is radical, embodying more than Shiva Shakti and the concept of blood flowing down and sperm shooting up. Our conditioning means we find the image of a woman, unapologetically conquering and dominating a man, to be revolutionary. This image of our Goddess ancestor, wielding such force, opens the door to conceptual freedom, from the bondage of patriarchy.

Kali steps upon Shiva, with right foot forward, the Dakshinachara, the right-hand path, of truth and balance. Rather than extolling the virtues of the right over left, or getting into the gunas, it is the act of stepping forward that is important. Step into your power; step into warrior pose; take baby steps; set your intention. Free yourself, be your own hero and never look back!

11) Reach Out To Community

Perhaps the image of Kali's skirt of many arms, symbolising action, in combination with her four arms, clutching her toolbox, can point us towards communal action, for there is strength in numbers. By joining forces, we are not alone. Healing should not be a solitary act. Together we can create momentum for change. Kali's many communal arms means more hugs; more hands for dispensing tissues; more wine; more ideas; more raised hands in support of change!

12) Harness Red Rage

In Kali iconography there is blood everywhere. She collects blood and drinks it – symbolic of her wisdom lineage and the forces that balance Nature. This is the blood of life – menstruation – the purifying, communal blood ritual, of cosmic, life giving, flow, that unites all women. Was this communal act sabotaged by patriarchy? Did they devise the 'communal act' of drinking Christ's blood, to steal female power?

Kali's eyes are described as red with delirium and rage – Red Rage! Women have every right to be angry, but often our anger gets hidden away, directed inwards, stuffed in the shadows. Our boundaries get crossed and we get angry, but this is not female rage. Female rage is the communal rage of social injustice. Harnessing Red Rage, as a communal act, can be a driving force for change. Surviving trauma can become a positive force, a 'gift to humanity', in the form of shared wisdom.

In her primordial form, before she was codified, Kali was worshipped as the raw spirit of Mother Nature – The Lady Of The Forest. Her free-flowing hair, blowing in the four cardinal directions – cartwheels in the hair – turned with the immense forces of cosmic motion. She is the Goddess of female emancipation, making her own rules, defying the rules society imposes on Her, including chastity!

Kali says, "Untamed Mother Nature is your hero. Seek abundance, commit to personal growth and keep on growing!"

I am Kali

Art and words by Kat Shaw

I am Kali.

Destroyer of the ego.

I am your mirror, your destruction, your self-realisation, your desperation, your devastation, your darkest nights, and your death.

But I am also your rebirth, your hope, the dawn of the morning, your mother.

Destroyer, preserver, and creator.

I am limitless. Clad in the colour of the universe. The womb of existence, the dance of time, the endless potential of creation. No finite dress can cover me as I dance amongst the stars. My nakedness is my sexuality. I am the nourisher of all beings with my abundant, voluptuous breasts. I am a woman in her own power – the embodiment of ferocious feminine energy.

With my dishevelled hair, flowing freely, I am a wild woman, breaking free from convention and all that holds me back. I am my own choices. I am fierce.

Fear the glistening when you see the blade of my enlightening sword because I do not fear to strike. I will sever the chords that link you to your ego and slay your most intrusive, toxic behaviours. With my strike I will release your soul forever from unnecessary delusions.

I wear my skull around my neck with pride, reminding me of battles, victims, obstacles and victories. The last dying breath of the ego.

My teeth, I bear as I snarl, looking fear directly in the face and howling – showing my tongue as a warning. I am always ready to fight for my highest good.

I am your Mother. The mother of all. My harsh discipline and severity, rage, and fury, are for your own good. Because, my child, I see your potential. I see what you can be, and I will fight for you. Always. I will nurture you with an unconditional loving embrace in your darkest hour, holding you close and rocking you until the light returns.

Look into my eyes my child... wild, awake, penetrating – blazing with the fires of intensity.

Look into my eyes because they are your eyes.

The eyes of a warrior.

Slip into my skin. Feel my soul because we are one. Merged.

Fearless and blessed.

We are in our power. Our own destinies.

I am you and you are me.

Sexual Abuse Healing Ritual

Annie Finch

In 2011, one third of women in the U.S. reported they had been victims of sexual assault (rape, stalking, beating, or a combination of assaults). If that definition were widened to include the far more common sorts of sexual abuse described in my first post, the percentage of us whose hearts have been damaged, voices silenced, and power shamed or weakened in some way by sexual abuse would, it seems safe to guess, approach close to 100%. And if that is the situation in the U.S., where women are in one of the strongest positions on the planet, imagine what it is in other parts of the world where women's rights are far more severely curtailed, voices far more severely shut down. There are so many of us, and each of us has our own fully unique healing path to follow.

Unfortunately for those of us who have experienced sexual abuse, it seems pretty clear that ignoring such an experience, no matter how long you ignore it, cannot make it go away. The repressed memories of times when you disassociated from your body and denied your emotions can drain away at your energy for years or decades. Healing from sexual abuse is essential work if we aim to live our lives fully, to share our gifts completely. The good news is that, as those of us who are in the midst of the healing process already know, healing *is* possible and can be quite a simple process.

As I am sure you have learned, no matter how much support we have, we must be the ones who heal ourselves, and no-one else can do this essential and intimate work for us. Yet we can also help each other—not only by speaking out but also by sharing what works. I designed the following ritual for my own healing, and I hope it will also be helpful to others, of any gender, who are trying to regain your power after incidents of sexual abuse or violation.

Please remember, as you do the ritual, if anything takes you out of the moment, it's fine to stop doing it. We all have different backgrounds and capacities for ritual, and since this is a ritual for *you alone,* its only value or point is what honestly works for you. If all you can do sincerely with this ritual is to sit on your couch and read it aloud, that's ok, since the most important thing is to be honest with yourself. But, that said, remember that ritual only comes alive and does its fullest work of communicating with your unconscious when it is performed and enacted *in your body.* So, acting it out will be most effective, and if you can only bring yourself to read it, be sure at least to say the words *aloud.*

A Ritual for Healing from Sexual Abuse

Prepare Yourself. Nurture yourself in the best way you feel called to do before the ritual. You could eat and sleep well, bathe, anoint yourself with oils, and/or connect with yourself spiritually through nature, an altar or meditation space, or an author or musician who nurtures you.

Label the Incidents (Optional). If you would like to prepare ahead, you could think about which incidents you want to heal from and which part of your body you remember them in. Then give each incident a label. Remember that you are not required to use the perpetrator's name or to think of them in any way; this not about them anymore. You are free to label the abusive experience from your own point of view, using words that resonate with *you* and hold only your own experience of the abuse. So, rather than naming an incident *"what xx made me do in his car,"* instead you could call it *"the penis-touching in the car"* or even *"the time my hand wasn't mine."* It's about *you* only. As an example, to heal from incidents in my life, I chose the labels *"I call back my power from "Joey wants your pussy.""* *I call back my power from the*

hand on the thigh." "I call back my power from the tongue in the mouth." "I call back my power from the rape in the eyes."
Or, you may not need to prepare at all. If you prefer to be completely spontaneous, it's fine to let all your words arise for the first time during the ritual itself. When in doubt, as always, proceed in the way that makes you feel happiest.

Prepare the Space. If possible, do the ritual alone in private, or in a group with people you completely trust. Make the space clear of clutter and warm enough so you will stay relaxed. It is best to be naked, or wearing a loose robe you can remove quickly if you want. Have a glass of water or a healing drink (such as nettle infusion) handy, and maybe a light shawl or scarf you can use for dancing or comfort. Before you begin, purify the place. Simple tools for this include scent (burning sage or incense, sprinkling essential oil), movement (dance, yoga or simple circling movements done with the intention to purify), and/or sound (a bell or chime, or simply your voice singing or saying, "this is a safe space").   Take all the time you need to make sure you will really feel safe here.

PART 1: Take Your Power Back and Invite in the Earth

Stand in the prepared space. Raise your left arm, and slowly turn counterclockwise.* For each incident (or group of incidents) you want to cleanse, feel the energy in your left hand, focus on the incident, and refer to it by its label, saying, *"I call back my power from xx"* as you bring your hand down to touch the affected part of your body.

As you move your hand to the part of your body that experienced the abuse, feel your rightful power coming back in and making you whole. Notice the healing energy in your hand as you do this. Each time, savor the feeling of having your thigh, mouth, eyes, hand, vulva, etc. back again. Take your time and allow yourself to be completely healed. Your left hand, and your whole body, may feel very warm.

Now use the warm energy you have raised to pull up into yourself the essence of the earth mother who cleanses and recycles all things. Let the earth energy fill you and heal any remaining hurt. You can repeat the chant below to help pull up the energy, using *"Earth," "Mother Earth,"* or names of specific Earth goddesses from around the world. Swaying or moving your body in time to the chant gives it more power. As you chant, feel the earth energy entering through your feet and rising through your body, making you whole and connected.

> *Goddess mother earth,*
> *I fill up myself with your beautiful power.*
> *I fill up my body with your love and your giving.*

Or

> *Goddess mother earth,*
> *Pacha Mama, Demeter, Asase Yaa, Freya,*
> *Danu, Mago, Gaia, Nu Gua .*
> *I fill up myself with your beautiful power.*
> *I fill up my body with your love and your giving.*

When you have chanted enough and feel healed and whole, open your hands above your head (like spreading your branches out in tree pose in yoga), and feel the beauty of your restored power as a gift you can share. By sharing, you complete the cycle and open yourself to receive more power.
Say,

> *I offer my power to the universe now.*
> *I offer my power, I'm full and I'm whole.*
> *I offer my mind, body, heart, will, and soul.*

PART 2: Love Your Wounding Now it is time to revisit the truth of your pain from the place of wholeness.

Get close to the earth: kneel, go into child's pose from yoga, or lie down, and say,

> *I've been broken, I've been bent*
> *I've been twisted, I've been turned*
> *I've been hurt, I've been burned*
> *And I rise in my body*
> *I rise in my perfection.*

Now come up onto your knees, and touch your body if you want to. Experience how perfect it is, like a gorgeous tree that has been bent by its experiences into a unique, strong, and perfect shape. Say,

I rise in my perfection and my power
Stand up completely and keep repeating
I rise in my beauty, my perfection, and my peace
I am bent and I am perfect
I am wounded, I am perfect
I accept, I release

Keep dancing and chanting
I am wounded, I am perfect
I accept, I release

If you have a light shawl or scarf you can dance with it at this point as you repeat the chant.

If, as you love yourself in these ways, a feeling of grief comes over you, that's fine. Your pain is real and true, and you dishonor yourself if you bargain it away or minimize it. At the same time, though, you don't need to let it take over. You might simply salute it, feeling free to acknowledge its size and strength. If there is a part of your body that is hurting, damaged, or broken in a physical way from what you have experienced, now do a freestyle movement with your body (like in yoga when you stretch freely) as you chant, again,

I am wounded
I am perfect
I accept
I release

Dance freely, touch yourself, contort, express your body. Play with your voice, as you say the chant.

Be angry, ugly, sarcastic, bitter, violent, reverent, triumphant, all the feelings that come through for you. Touch any part of your body as long as you like, with affection, fury, shame, grief. Claim it all. It is *yours* now. Your body. Exactly as it is. It's all yours!

And it is perfect.

Channel animals if you like. The hissing snake, the roaring tiger, the soaring eagle, the steady turtle, the running antelope, the confident wolf. Use sound effects, noises, and rhythms, anything that helps you express your power.

Continue until you feel fully powerful.

When you feel you are ready, you can put the scarf over your head and then pull it down to your shoulders like a robe of power as you speak the chant for the last time.

Now give yourself a "grandmother hug" (this was passed on to me from Deborah E'llelia who learned it from a group of spiritual grandmothers in Hawaii, powerful women who don't rely on others for validation): Cross your arms in front of you and put your hands on the opposite shoulders, patting both shoulders simultaneously as you tell yourself, "good job!" three times.

PART 3: Coming Back Into Your Center With Your Web of Power

Women gain strength from our connections with one another; our levels of the magnificent hormone oxytocin rise when we are with other women. So, the final step of the ritual is to ground our healing within the witnessing embrace of a circle of supportive others—a web of power. (If you have been doing the ritual in a group, you have three options: skip this step since your healing has been witnessed; continue while the people around you support you in creating your inner web of power; or pause and continue with Part 3 later, when you're alone.)

When you are ready to weave a web of power around your newly-healed self, stand in the center of your ritual space and look around. Feel the warmth of your heart pulsing with its amazing capacity to create love and connection. Feel your ability to bring into a beautiful, vibrant, supportive circle those who will love, support and honor your new, whole way of being.

Slowly reach out and, one by one (alternating hands work well for this), pull the people you want to support you into your circle. As you choose each person, say, "I pull into my center _____" and call out their name.

Those you call in can be friends, colleagues, heroines, ancestors, role models, children, goddesses or other deities, or even animals. If no-one comes to mind, just keep repeating, "I pull into my center _____" until more names come to you. Pull in as many names as you are called to; somewhere between 3 and 20 is probably a good number. The main thing is that each of the people you pull in should feel completely fabulous.

Remember, only pull in people with whom you feel completely safe and who you feel strengthen you and are on your side. Even people you love very much who don't fit in this category should be left outside your web of power. Your web of power is about people who will completely support your new, healed self — not about love per se.

If you are a woman, you may want to give extra thought before pulling any men into your center space, your web of power. Men can be extremely loving and helpful in our lives from a slightly peripheral place, and they tend to be OK with this. There can be great value in a women-only space, especially when it comes to healing from sexual abuse. It is in no way an insult to a man if you want to reserve your center for supportive females only. Similarly, you may love one of your female family members very much, but if she eats at you even a little bit, she does not belong in your web of power. Be scrupulously honest. Your inner life is at stake.

If you do call in someone and then change your mind, you can always undo it at any time by turning clockwise and saying, "I release you from my center" [yes, I meant clockwise; as a woman I find that the moon-wise, counterclockwise direction builds and strengthens me. I use clockwise for the rare times I am undoing or releasing something]. Say it emphatically, emphasizing the rhythm, as many times as needed until you feel they are no longer in your web of power.

When you have called in everyone and are feeling happy and jazzed and released, flooded with oxytocin at the thought of the great supportive people in your web of power, chant:

> *"Circle of power, circle around me,*
> *Web of power, hold me strong.*
> *I am in my web of power,*
> *Circle around me, circle around me."*

Your web of power will be with you always. You will never need to be alone.

Thanks and Closing

1. Hug yourself, pat yourself on the shoulders, and say "good job"! Tap your hands together once and hold them there as you thank yourself, by name.
2. Hold your hands in prayer position and thank the room for containing your healing.
3. Hold your hands on your heart and give a final thanks to those in your web of power.
4. Now, hands outstretched or open, thank the goddess, god, earth, the universe, ancestors, totem animals, guiding spirit, or any other forces you feel moved to thank.
5. If you started by casting a circle, release it now.

Note: if you feel that turning the opposite way from the direction indicated, or using the opposite hand, is more effective for you, that's fine.

-

Blessings and love to all of you, to all of us, as we heal and grow and shine!

This ritual was originally shared on Annie's website – and we thank her for allowing us to share it with you here.

https://anniefinch.com/ritual-healing-sexual/

Illuminatrix
Kat's Shaw

Facing My Trauma as a Female Leader within Patriarchy

Dr Lynne Sedgmore

Introduction

I want to share both the suppressed and the overt trauma I have experienced in my journey of being a successful woman leader in a predominantly male environment, within our patriarchal society. I want also to articulate the importance of Goddess spirituality in healing that trauma.

I write this piece for any women who are simultaneously succeeding, as well as struggling in the world. I wish to support any woman leader unable to understand the depth of her own trauma, or to find the support, caring and self-nourishment she truly needs to feel fully whole, and to thrive within her leadership role. I use the word leader for someone who is in a responsible and accountable position within a community or organisation.

I am one of those women who always thought trauma involves other people, but not myself. Despite the various ups and downs in my life, I always put on a brave face, picked myself up; and carried on regardless. I was strong woman, brave woman, warrior woman fighting injustices and caring for others. I was autonomous and self-sufficient.

As well as successes, my career was littered with numerous deeply distressing and disturbing experiences. I did not experience acute or chronic trauma, but I definitely had complex trauma to the extent that I needed professional help.

Finding Goddess spirituality has been an incredibly liberating and nourishing experience for me. Feeling the presence of a female divinity enabled me to heal more deeply. I believe this is because I experience Goddess as a female energetic web with qualities of interconnection, love and holding within the world. These three qualities, experienced directly and viscerally, enable me to feel held and strong, as well as vulnerable and open. From this sacred space and inner knowing, I can go deep into my feelings of anxiety, unknowing, struggle and confusion to understand myself, and others, more clearly.

Loving Goddess has freed me to go further into my mother and sister wounding, and to face, to a whole new level, my complex trauma, and the reality, of external and internal patriarchy.

In 2017 I created the Goddess Luminary Leadership Wheel – a Goddess centred leadership development programme which challenges the patriarchal leadership paradigm. My course has included several students who skillfully know and own their own trauma. I have learnt SO much from them. Also, by travelling more deeply into my understanding and expression of power I am now able to fully face and own my own trauma.

Context

I worked in Further Education (FE), within the English educational system, for over 36 years. It is a very male dominated vocational learning environment. In 1984, I decided that I wanted to have positional power within the hierarchy of an FE college in order to support and liberate myself, and other women. I was promoted many times from being a lecturer in 1980 until I became a college principal in 1998. For 17 years I was a chief executive in three different organisations.

I was genuinely trying to make the world a better place and to transform the lives of students through being a leader in FE colleges. I felt successful, satisfied and fulfilled, and really felt I was making a positive difference to the lives, education and well-being of thousands of students and staff. I was driven to change the existing college sexist culture and to play my part, as a feminist and Goddess loving woman, in bringing about gender equality and progress.

And I did – I can give you hundreds of examples of championing and implementing equality and diversity alongside supporting women into leadership roles and making their lives within further education organisations a lot better; but that's a different article.

I learnt how to traverse the college system to achieve and what I wanted to. I always made sure my teams, and myself, over-delivered so we had autonomy and space to experiment, innovate and challenge the negative aspects of bureaucracy. I became known as the "enemy of bureaucracy lovers everywhere" and sat on the national FE anti-bureaucracy task force. I created what I called oasis of sanity and autonomy for my teams. I protected them from the worst ravages of erratic national policy confetti and unnecessary rigid rules.

I stayed in FE for 36 years because I knew that my quirks and rebellions would be tolerated while allowing me to make significant differences, impact, and achievements.

What did trauma have to do with me? Trauma was for other people, those unable to cope with life. It had nothing to do with a successful chief executive, especially one with a successful track record, a CBE honours from the Queen, and several national and international awards.

I equated trauma with weakness, and I was the strong one. How wrong I was in this perspective and belief.

Suppressed trauma

Alongside my success, I was also highly stressed and experienced many obstacles and difficulties as a senior female leader. I was frequently the only woman on senior college teams, sometimes treated as the token woman.

The price of my success involved feeling I had always to perform better than the men around me, especially on the occasions that I was the only senior woman leader in an otherwise all male team. The huge effort involved in constantly trying to be superwoman – the good mother, the good wife, the outstanding person, never making a mistake, always presenting myself as the high achieving professional. I often felt an outsider, and was treated as other, or lesser than, the men – by many male colleagues. I rebelled by wearing flowery, feminine frocks and not adapting to the corporate style by becoming one of the grey suits.

To survive, and especially to thrive, I had to accommodate and live with active, unwanted, unsolicited sexism on a daily basis. I challenged the sexist comments, the uninvited touching of my body, the dreadful sexist jokes, being interrupted in mid sentence and my verbal contributions ignored or taken by men as their own. I was frequently called aggressive when I was being genuinely assertive. I learnt to accommodate and challenge, just enough, but not too much to draw active hostility, rejection or ejection from the organisation.

The phrase micro aggressions wasn't around at the early stages of my career, but my everyday life as a female leader was full of sexual and sexist micro aggressions. Initially I challenged every single occasion of these because it felt the right feminist response. I also wanted to be a role model to other women, in less senior posts, of the importance of calling out all shapes and forms of sexism. It was absolutely exhausting. The gaslighting, denial and male aggression to my challenges didn't stop me, but I was acutely aware that over the years I began to underplay some of what was happening to me because I needed to focus my energy on other things. What did happen was the more senior, and the more skillful I became in challenging sexism, the less I experienced overt and damaging sexism.

Yet patriarchal sexism was always present in some shape or form. It was endemic, systemic, and rife. Constant sexism, while being treated as a normal and acceptable status quo by your male colleagues, is a draining, de-energising situation that wears you down. You begin to feel like the "humourless, aggressive feminist" they accuse you of being; especially when you speak out too much for their liking.

I've always been an emotional overeater and carried excess weight, but overall, my health was really good and I hardly had any days from work off sick. Instead of seeing my disordered eating as a symptom of trauma, I went on and off diets to control my weight. It's only in my later years that I have been able to work through my complex eating patterns to create a healthier relationship with food.

I now understand that the need to be strong and overly independent, alongside an inability to receive support from others, is a trauma response. A survival tactic to protect my heart from abuse, neglect, betrayal, and disappointment. I was the woman who coped with sexism and patriarchal toxicity through being task orientated and denying my own hurt and distress. I pushed my emotions down and carried on regardless. I rescued others instead of looking to my own needs.

Overt trauma

Eventually, I had to face just how horrible it really was working within the constraints, demands and challenges of a patriarchal leadership system. I began to realise how little space there was for

153

my fullest expression as a woman leader or for my self-nourishment amidst the ongoing relentless pace of work and organisational demands.

By 1990 I was flailing, so I chose to go into therapy to cope personally with the difficulties I was facing; both externally and internally. I needed time and space to explore my professional issues, and to understand and work through the complexities of being a woman leader in a predominantly male environment. I began to read books on trauma, shadow, projection and toxic leadership. I found female networks of other women struggling in similar ways. We co-created beautiful spaces of support as like-minded women who supported me on my journey. Several remain my friends 30 years later.

To undertake the internal work, I needed to do I had to find a deep source of strength to sustain me. This included my spirituality, as well as my feminism.

Goddess played a huge role in my recovery. My first opening to Goddess was when I experienced the landscape as female during a women only residential writing retreat. It was a life changing experience. In seeing the female face of the Divine, I felt my womanhood as viscerally sacred, I experienced myself as already whole – a hugely significant realisation. I visited ancient Greek Goddess sites and temples, including Delphi, to soak up Her energy. Goddess enabled me to see clearly how I had still internalised aspects of patriarchy, even though I has been a feminist since 1967, and had actively fought against sexism and for equality and women's liberation as a second wave feminist.

When I left the FE system in 2015, only then could I fully allow, understand, and integrate the depth of the trauma that patriarchy imposes on all women, including woman leaders, every single day of our working life. I needed time to repair, heal, and restore.

So, what is this full-blown sense of trauma that I now feel?

In 2017, I gave a talk at Huddersfield University on toxic leadership, my own, and that of others. I talked passionately, honestly, and openly about how toxic leadership had affected me on a spiritual, emotional, and physical level. I owned my own shadow and toxicity as well as speaking publicly about the harm, sexism, and distress I had experienced from others. The positive response and recognition of similar experiences from other FE women was humbling and very moving. After I delivered this lecture I came home and sobbed. I cried for days, re-experiencing all the hurt that I'd never allowed myself to feel so fully before.

Conclusion

It is only in hindsight that I truly understand the depth and impact of the trauma I experienced working within our patriarchal organisations, systems and society. All of which significantly disadvantage and traumatise generally, and target women who step into formal leadership roles.

Since 2015, I have ensconced myself even more deeply in Goddess spirituality by training as a Priestess of Avalon alongside teaching my Goddess Luminary Leadership Wheel. I take part in Goddess ceremonies with the Glastonbury Goddess Temple and live in Glastonbury to be part of the Avalonian Goddess tradition and community. Goddess is my core spiritual path and sustenance.

I am grateful, every day for the experience and blessings of Goddess in my life, especially for the understanding, healing, and holding of my suppressed and overt trauma over the past 40 years.

Blessed Be.

Swimming a Witch

Donna Gerrard

The daughter of a mother met me in a circle of stone
Clad in yellow
Dark of skin
She invited me to follow her home.
The water was my tears of joy.

The journey took me to a white spring
Clad in rags
Dirty of skin
They invited me to sit on a stool.
The water was my piss of fear.

That journey took me down, down in dark waters
Clad in a shift
Ears filled with laughter
They invited my body back onto the bank.
The water was in my lungs.

That journey took me towards the light
Clad in white wings
Cleansed of skin
She invited me to fly on a swan
The water was far, far below me.

The journey took me to a dark spring
Clad in yellow
Tingling of skin
She invited to join my waters with hers.
The water was our womb.

The daughter of a mother met me in a chapel of stone
Clad in yellow
Dark of skin
She welcomed me home.
The water was my tears of joy.

This poem is the story of my initiation into the divine feminine traditions, starting with encountering Saint Sarah, daughter of Mary Magdalene, in a shamanic journey to meet one of our guides. I had never even heard of her before that day, and that shamanic journey initiated me onto a path with both the Rose lineage and the Brighde-Brigantia traditions, through re-living a past life memory of being drowned as a witch (the practice known as 'swimming a witch'), being taken up on a swan towards the light by Goddess, and finally meeting Saint Sarah again when I was meditating in Glastonbury Abbey on the weekend of my Rose lineage initiation. It's my soul story of healing from patriarchal abuse through the grace of Goddess.

I am Your Darkness
Words and Art by Kat Shaw

I am your darkness.
Your stillness.
Your void.
Your poison.
Your hollowness.
Your emptiness.
Your nothingness.
Your abyss.
Your unsaid words.
Your dead dreams.
Your secrets.
Your silence.

I am an integral part of you.
As worthy as your light.
Embrace me.
Step in to being whole.

Healing Dreams

Trista Hendren

I am no stranger to trauma.

I wish I had been dealt a different hand, but there is no changing the past. All I can do is focus on my own healing and try to ensure that my children and grandchildren do not have to carry my trauma.

The insidious thing about abuse is that it teaches you to continue to mistreat yourself long after the abuser is out of your life—so you are effectively continuing to do his work for him. Clarissa Pinkola Estés explained this phenomenon well:

> "If a woman has had a difficult upbringing—if she has had emotional, spiritual, or physical trauma in her life— assaults to inner, creative or active life—these cause the predator to manifest itself as a loud and brittle critic, as accuser and ambusher within the psyche. Thereafter, each time a woman attempts to achieve a hope or a dream, each time she strives for something new, the natural predator—now grown large—will attempt to defeat her by both disparaging her and wreaking havoc with her plans."[11]

It took me many decades to break ties with my predator—and to stop interacting with other predators. I had to literally re-wire my brain so that I would begin to treat myself kindly—and have zero tolerance for people who treat me poorly.

---

11 Estés, Clarissa Pinkola. Ph.D. *Women Who Run with The Wolves – Contacting the Power of the Wild Woman.* Random House; 1993.

Michelle Rosenthal wrote, "Trauma creates change you don't choose. Healing is about creating change you do choose."[12] Healing begins when we realize that there are other ways of doing things—other ways of being. While most of us repeat the patterns of our family of origin, we do not have to.

For most of my life, I spoke to myself horribly. When I decided that I must stop doing that, my life began to change enormously. While I still slip on occasion, I try to treat myself with loving kindness now—and have filled my life with people who do the same.

This is another reason inner-child work can be very effective. I often think about 'little Trista' as a small child and hold her in my heart. I have learned to speak to her with love and compassion.

Like many trauma warriors, I have tried almost everything to heal myself. I have spent many decades desperately trying to heal myself.

What seems like the best method to me at this point in my life, is to stop trying so hard—and to rest.

Those of us with high ACE scores are much more likely to become seriously ill and die early.[13] Those of us with childhood trauma need to take better care of ourselves than most people.

Therefore, extreme self-care and proper sleep must become high priorities.

Sleep is something you should never be stingy with, but most people don't get enough of it. As I get older, I have noted that I really do not function well without 8 solid hours.

---

12 Rosenthal, Michelle *Your Life After Trauma: Powerful Practices to Reclaim Your Identity*. W. W. Norton & Company; 2015.

13 van der Kolk, Bessel M.D. *The Body Keeps the Score: Brain, Mind, and Body in the Healing of Trauma*. Penguin Publishing Group; Reprint edition, 2015.

I still have some unresolved trauma remaining in my body, so sleep is sometimes difficult for me—particularly if there is any additional stress in my life at the moment. My life is not in chronic stress-mode like it used to be—but I can default to that if something triggers me, and I let it go unchecked.

I have found that keeping a bottle of lavender essential oil is helpful to me during the night if I wake up. I also can reset myself by touching my husband or dog—connecting to some of their energy. Most nights, my husband gives me a full body massage beforehand to relax into the night. A cup of tea or a hot bath are also good rituals. Anything you can do to create a nighttime ritual to let your body know it is time to sleep will help you sleep better.

Good sleep has become one of my top priorities. I used to view it as a waste of time, but now I enjoy sleeping. I absolutely love my bed and I stay in it as long as I possibly can each morning.

Getting enough sleep also has allowed me to heal areas of my life that I was not able to confront earlier in my life. As someone who has had a lot of nightmares, I loved Anthony William's perspective:

> "Bad' dreams are the soul's way of healing. When we're awake, we're not supposed to be breaking down the walls of our emotional hurt. When we are wounded, a physical component in the brain puts up a barrier to prevent us from constantly processing and reprocessing the pain, so that we can be productive and move forward during our waking hours. They're not walls of denial; they're walls of divine protection. While some conscious processing is healthy and necessary, it's not meant to haunt us.
>
> The time to process that pain is in our sleep. When we're not conscious, the emotional walls come down so the soul can do its cleanup and repair work. This means that all sorts of difficult emotions get stirred up, and they work themselves out through our dreams. If this didn't happen,

frustration, anger, fear, betrayal, guilt, and humiliation would build up and up and up within us until they overpowered the strength of the walls holding them in place and took over our waking lives. Instead, our dreams release them. This nightly housecleaning—aided by the Angel of Sleep, the Angel of Dreams, and the Unknown Angels—helps us face what's going on in life without becoming scarred by it."[14]

When I wake up from a nightmare, I ground myself and acknowledge that I still have some trauma to process. And, that's OK. I comfort myself as I would one of my children awakening from a bad dream.

I was very close to all my grandparents, although my maternal grandfather died young as a result of his alcoholism. All of them still come to me in my dreams regularly. This has brought me peace around their deaths. Truth be told, I would have liked to have kept all of them around forever, but that is not how life unfolds.

Through dream work, I am also able to heal relationships that have been extraordinarily difficult. I have found forgiveness and acceptance toward my stepmother and my children's father. I have been able to see sides of their spirits that I was not able to while they were living.

It is frustrating that we repeat familial patterns that we already have seen do not work out well—almost as if they were encoded in our DNA. I vividly remember my Pappa's alcoholic rages toward other family members during my childhood. It did not stop me from marrying an alcoholic, who took out his rage on me.

---

14 William, Anthony. *Thyroid Healing: The Truth behind Hashimoto's, Graves', Insomnia, Hypothyroidism, Thyroid Nodules & Epstein-Barr.* Hay House Inc.; June 1, 2021.

I remember sitting down with my maternal grandmother when my children were young and asking her what I should do about my marriage. I knew she would understand like no one else. She had lived it.

There was sadness in her eyes when she told me that I should leave if I could. Looking back at her life, with 5 children by the age of 22—she had no choice, but to stay.

"Choice" is still a relative term for most women.

Eventually, I did choose to leave. But I paid dearly for that choice.[15]

Acceptance has always been a difficult concept for me. I have often wished things were different than they were, which has often resulted in me seeing horrible situations with rose-colored glasses.

Cheryl Strayed's passage on the subject is my all-time favorite.

> "Most things will be okay eventually, but not everything will be. Sometimes you'll put up a good fight and lose. Sometimes you'll hold on really hard and realize there is no choice but to let go. Acceptance is a small, quiet room."[16]

I sat with this passage a lot both before and after my children's father died at the young age of 45.

I did not find peace with him until after his death. While I am not one to preach forgiveness to women, it was healing for me to let go of all my anger toward him. This world was a very hard place for him, too. We both had deep childhood wounds. Through dreaming, I have been able to mend some of that.

15 Hendren, Trista. *Hearts Aren't Made of Glass: My Journey from Princess of Nothing to Goddess of My Own Damned Life*. Girl God Books; 2016.
16 Strayed, Cheryl. Tiny Beautiful Things: Advice on Love and Life from Dear Sugar. Knopf Doubleday Publishing Group; 2012.

In her groundbreaking book, *Patriarchy Stress Disorder,* Dr. Valerie Rein wrote:

> "Ancestral trauma does not spring from the events in our own lives, and yet we carry it with us and pass it along to the next generations—until we heal it. This trauma does not 'belong to us' individually, but it shapes how each one of us shows up in the world today. When we heal it, we end the cycle of trauma transmission, liberating not only ourselves, but the future generations."[17]

A therapist once told me that when you grow up traumatized, it is not unusual to become addicted to drama. *It's what you know.* It took me a long time to crave peace and happiness instead. I hope that is what my children will also look for.

I leave you with this closing thought from Anthony William:

> "We wish each other 'sweet dreams,' when really, we should wish each other 'healing dreams.' To advance the soul, mend the heart, and empty yourself of harmful emotions, you don't want every dream to be perfect and tranquil and flowery. You don't want your dream life to be an all-out wonderland. You want your dreams to have some hardship in them, because you want the good stuff to be happening when you're awake. If our dream lives were total fantasy, sleeping would be the only thing we'd want to do."[18]

May you find deep healing in your dreams.

---

17 Rein, Valerie. Ph.D. *Patriarchy Stress Disorder*: the Invisible Inner Barrier to Women's Happiness and Fulfillment. Lioncrest Publishing; 2019.

18 William, Anthony. *Thyroid Healing: The Truth behind Hashimoto's, Graves', Insomnia, Hypothyroidism, Thyroid Nodules & Epstein-Barr.* Hay House Inc.; June 1, 2021.

Reclaiming the Goddess

Barbara O'Meara

Dark Feminine ~ The Morrigan Speaks

Kathy Barenskie

I am the Gypsy Priestess
Wild Woman
Triple Deity
Shape Shifter and Crone.
I am the Morrigan
Man, Woman.
 I am every One of You who dare to dream to be whole again.
So Integrate Me
    Embrace Me
    Breathe Me in
    Love Me
For I am all the dark parts of you.

Do not fear me.
For I will not stand in the doorway, be the good wife and mother
to the offspring of your nothingness as did Macha.
Nor will I curse you as did she in some passive act of anger.
Not that from me!
For I am not a victim
As was she.
I am the Warrior Goddess.

Ah, but a warning to you Father, Brother, Son.
Deny me and I will hunt you down, to sit as a Crow on the
shoulder of your corpse.
This I did to the hero Cú Chulainn.
Ah, yet do not fear me,
Come bathe with me instead
in the cool waters of uncertainty.
As I did with my consort the Dagda
There I will hold you in the sacred void.

We will join in union.

The death I offer is but a catalyst for life.
I am here to lift that curse of Macha
with open body.
My cold winters are a dark magic of loveless lust.
For the sacredness of my black soil is where the seeds of true life
are planted.
So do not fear me,
I usher in prophecy and new beginnings.
Embrace my fierce Femininity.

And you Women,
Love your darkness.
You are not all sugar,
  all spice.
Love Your Shadow,
for That is your strength.
Instead, channel me,
for I have seen your magic.
The real magic that all women do.
In simple acts.

Transforming a house into a home.
Adding colour, comfort and warmth where once was none.
Loving the grey into rainbows with heart and frills.
Turning basic into comfort adorned.
Heart hearthstone

I've seen the healing.
The real healing that only women do.
Sharing a cup of tea and company.
Giving of their sweetness in words that empower.
Swapping bitter nouns for kindness and a cup of honey.
To sweeten a life.

I've seen the Beauty.
The real beauty that only women own.
Miraculous bodies birth Spirit into this world.
Changing with age as gravity pulls. Yet growing more beautiful
with greys and skin wrinkled and silver swirled.

Softness and full bodies.
Everlasting blessed beauty
I've seen the Wisdom.
The real wisdom that only women have.
Wisdom shared from the Hidden.
Blessings abundant.

I am the Morrigan
And I am every One of You who dare to dream to be whole again.
So Integrate Me
    Embrace Me
    Breathe Me
    Love Me
For I am the dark parts of all of you."

The Morrigan

Kat Shaw

Holy Affliction

Lori Santo

In the deepest, darkest crevices of my embodiment
My cells carry the voices of the Ancients' attunement
Right alongside volcanic fires of my Spirit's guidance
To hold on, not let go, the Holy Grail of my True Essence
My trauma informed nervous system ripening on the cusp
Alchemizing all polarization, my body's Holy Wisdom is where I lay
my trust
My circuitry and cellular structure overarching all my divisions
A gift of my Highest Nature, redefining each of my multiple
dimensions
No denying the depths of the cauldron that created me
She comes from everywhere I am, stripping every falsity so that I
might See
And clear the path to poet my way through my own intimate
history
I lay crosses down in the dungeons to reshape my destiny
With lightning rod precision, my brilliance comes calling
From the dark slumbers that prefer more conformed numbing
She will never let me go... She's relentless in her quaking
Commanding me awake from my inertia, I wake trembling,
shaking
From her fiery, fierce commitment to my highest integrity
To answer the Call, scribed eons ago, to be written only by me
My Holy affliction is my genius as a Divine derelict
Leaving me awestruck by my body's piercing, Sacred Intellect.

Hecate

Kat Shaw

My Path to Hekate and Healing

Roxanne Rhoads

In early 2019 I started on a holistic path to healing from trauma, both my trauma and generational trauma. I started with a meditation class.

One of my early assignments was to meditate on who am I. I had so many problems with it. Every time I would meditate with the question "who am I?" the answer I received was Darkness. That scared me! I mean who wants to hear that they are Darkness? I felt like I was doing something wrong. So, I kept trying. But Darkness was always the answer...

Why did I have such a hard time accepting that I am Darkness? I've always been drawn to the darker side of life – ghosts and paranormal stuff, and all things spooky. I love the Goth aesthetic. I love dark beauty. My favorite colors are black and red, and my favorite holiday is Halloween so I shouldn't be surprised when the answer to "who am I?" turned out to be Darkness. I don't revel in the light. I'm not a creature of sunshine and beaches. I like Moonlight and Darkness and shadows.

But society as a whole has opinions about "darkness".

Darkness, especially feminine darkness along with feminine power has been portrayed by the patriarchy and modern society as something evil. Look at fairy tales and Disney movies – the evil stepmother, the evil queen, so many villains are powerful women. Look to recent politics. Hillary, AOC, Gretchen Whitmer the current Governor of Michigan – all women who have been demonized for being strong and fighting against oppression and patriarchal values.

The vilification of powerful women goes all the way to the roots of patriarchal religions. Women were once worshiped as the mother of all, as Goddesses of earth and nature, the essence of life itself. A balance was seen between the divine feminine and the divine masculine. But patriarchy took hold and turned Goddesses into demons, made powerful women something to be feared not revered. And the ego of men took over.

I grew up in this ego-driven world, taught that I should be meek and subservient to men. Not that I ever fit that mold very well. I grew up in a female household with my mother and grandmother. All the men in our life had passed away so it was just us. Other men came and went, but the women of our family ran the show, which could be why most men didn't stay.

But no matter who ran my household, men still ran the world, and that conditioning was in my head. Television, fashion magazines, movies, subtle messages ingrained into my brain from the very beginning. That conditioning made me question myself and my life.

My first serious boyfriend wanted me to be this cutesy feminine girl with blonde hair that wore pink. That wasn't me but I tried to be what he wanted, I bleached my hair and wore pretty pink things. But I wasn't good at being something I wasn't. Not even when he tried beating it into me. That rejection and failure stayed with me.

Other boyfriends continued to have problems with me. They hated my power, my uniqueness, me. I was labeled a "bitch". I was told to not be so dark. To lighten up. Literally. I was told to ditch the dark lipstick and black clothes. I needed to fit in. Not stand out.

So, there I was in forties meditating on being "darkness". I had to overcome all the negativity and trauma associated with my "darkness" that had been pushed into my brain and beat into my body for four decades.

After many meditations, I realized that Darkness and Light must coexist for balance. While I knew this to be true, being told "you are Darkness" repeatedly can feel ominous. But I finally started accepting it. As I accepted who I was, my life started getting better. Pieces started to fall into place.

Soon after my meditation assignment, I was talking to some of my witchy friends, and one mentioned a book she was reading. The book features keys being used in spells and different magical workings. In the book, keys are cleansed like crystals.

The mention of keys turned a key inside me and opened a door to the knowledge of my Darkness.

I have always had this self-imposed title "The Keeper of the Keys". This was something I gave myself as a child because it sounded magickal and mysterious. Throughout my life, I've collected keys even though I had no purpose for them. A couple of years ago I started doing some crafts and framing some of the prettier keys, but I still have tons of keys that I've never really done anything with other than stick them in boxes and jars.

Keys combined with my owl animal totem are symbols of the Goddess Hekate. Symbols that connect me to her.

Hekate is known as "The Keeper of the Keys". And here's another kicker – her colors are red, black, and white... anyone who knows me knows this has been my color combination since I was 15. My bedroom is even red, black, and white.

Most spiritual New Agers of love and light push Hekate deeper into the shadows because she is the goddess of Darkness, the night, the moon, magic, and witchcraft. She is so many things... including the embodiment of the triple Goddess – Maiden, Mother, Crone, and many find her too ominous to work with. Some push Hekate to the side because she is not sunshine and rainbows, light and love, peace, and tranquility. However, there are many Pagans and Witches who embrace her, darkness and all. I soon learned that She is much more than Darkness.

Her symbols have personally been part of my life for as long as I can remember and when I learned that the owl and keys are connected to Hekate it helped me feel like I finally found my way and accepted my path of Darkness.

Once I discovered Hekate I started doing shadow work. And by shadow work I mean it was time to do a really deep dig into my darker self, my past, and my trauma. Dig deep into the parts of me I find hard to deal with, the things I tell no one, the things I don't let out. Finding when and where things went wrong. Digging into my timeline and pinpointing the sources of trauma.

Hekate is the perfect goddess for shadow work. Dr. Cyndi Brannen, the author of *Keeping Her Keys*, has guided meditations available for Death Walking and Soul Retrieval among other things. These are deep dives into shadow work and soul repair.

Another thing that draws me to Hekate is that she is the goddess of liminal spaces, the crossroads, the goddess of the in-between, sunrise and sunset, Dusk and Dawn, shores and shorelines, places that are neither here nor there. And this may be the thing that resonates with me most of all because I have always felt neither here nor there like I didn't belong in any box or any space that is commonly defined. I was born on September 21st which can either be the last day of summer or the first day of fall depending on the yearly calendar. It's an in-between space because the weather can go either way it can still be 80° and sunny or it can be cold and rainy.

I was born right after midnight at 12:42 AM. Morning but not. The beginning of a new day yet still the Darkness of night. I'm on the Virgo and Libra cusp. I have mostly Virgo tendencies. I'm very organized. I'm a perfectionist but my Libra stands out from time to time because I do love beautiful things, I love giving gifts, I love art and music and books.

Discovering Hekate made me realize that she had been calling to me all my life, but I didn't have the tools or knowledge to hear her. Hekate came to me when I needed her most. In March 2019 my world was rocked with health news that could have broken me. But Hekate was there. She helped me go on. She guided me through all that Darkness, through the darkest time of my life, through a battle for my life and then again through the hell of my mother's death in 2021.

I keep honoring her by learning about her. The best sources I've found so far are KeepingHerKeys.com and Dr. Cyndi Brannen's books.

Before Hekate, I honored The God and The Goddess, not any specific god or goddess other than Ariadne, who came to me when I was a young teenager. Some may argue she is not a Goddess but a guide. And guide me through those years she did. It wasn't until Hekate made herself known to me that I had a specific deity to devote myself to all the time. She opened my eyes to the world of Gods and Goddesses communicating with me and being there for me.

Since I became aware of Her, others have come to me with messages and have been there for me in times of need.

But I will never forget it was Hekate who helped me overcome societal conditioning and the trauma of abuse. It was Hekate who healed my body and soul when I was ill, and it was Hekate who used her torches to guide me back to the world of the living when I wanted to sink into the Underworld with my mother. Thank you, Hekate, for shining the light of your torches on my life.

Mother of Medusa

Alorah Welti

It was on the night
I was building an altar to ineffability
that I saw the moon on the wax,
weighted down by her ivory spine,
sink to the bottom of the night basin
like a stone.

Birth is a thick and sticky thing,
the root of everything unnamed and made.
When I could still remember the sounds of my mother's womb
I knew the songs, stories and the symbols.
After that, I was always reaching
in hollow communion,
searching for something I could not find.

That night,
I could see it in the corner of my eye,
taste it on the tip of my tongue.
I could feel the stirrings of
my unborn bird of prey,
held in the bowl of my pelvis
reciting all the forgotten omens,
thrumming the way ghosts do.

Just before dawn,
I was naked and moaning and covered in blood,
and my hair still smelled of the river Lethe.
Possessed with the sacredness of birth giving,
I passed through a boundary that is hard to define
and for a moment I had all of it –
so much truth and power that it poured out of me,
and then she was born.

My daughter, a fully formed winged woman,
stood before me, anointed in my blood.
In her eyes I could see that
she was whole, unfragmented.
Nothing had been taken from her.
The Mysteries had been promised to her
now and forever
and in that moment, and in every moment after,
her name reverberated within me
as a call to something greater:
Medusa, Medusa, Medusa.

Medusa's Scream III

Claire Dorey

Prisoner of War

Michelle Bear

The cage clangs shut.
No reprieve today.
There is no beginning.
Nor does it ebb, it only flows.

From new moon to full,
She alone bore witness.

To the sharp scalpel used.
Seconds, turn into weeks,
and then years of slow dissection.
Leaving me picked apart, eviscerated,
And unidentifiable.

From new moon to full,
She alone bore witness.

To the absent screams suffocating my voice.
Silence has been seared into my core.
No tears, no cries, nor confessions were ever heard.

From new moon to full,
She alone bore witness.

In December 2012, I underwent major pelvic surgery. My surgeon had stated it was "criminal" that the prolapsing of my bladder, vagina and uterus had been allowed to deteriorate to its current physical state. I needed surgery to remove my uterus and repair my vagina and bladder. What this surgeon proceeded to do to me was the true crime. The trans-vaginal mesh was eroding through my colon when it was supposed to be attached to my vagina. The wrong sutures had been used in my bladder and were eroding through my bladder tissue. Finally, I had necrotizing plugs of tissue

181

in my sacrum from more incorrect suture material rotting in my body. I almost lost my bladder, and I almost lost my life. I did suffer from intractable nerve pain in five different locations for more than six years. After three more surgeries, twenty-four procedures, and countless alternative treatments, I have been experiencing decreasing pain the last four years but increasing PTS (Post Traumatic Stress). Considering I was told I needed to be in a wheelchair, and I would spend the rest of my life in bed with incurable pain, I am now a living "medical miracle".

The worst loss was losing my voice. I was neglected, ignored, abused, and marginalized by the very people who were supposed to be my professional peers. I even took this surgeon to court, and it went all the way to trial. Not that I won the trial. I lost for a number of reasons. First, I was punished for being a nurse, apparently, I should never have let the surgeon botch my surgery. Again, because I was a nurse, I was told I should have diagnosed what was wrong with me. Thirdly, I was told I was too stoic. So, does that mean hysteria would have been preferable? Finally, the all-female jury determined the surgeon shouldn't have to lose his license, but apparently, it's acceptable I'll never work as a nurse again.

This poem is part of my healing inspired by my goddess, Macha. For almost a decade I have suffered in silence, but I was never alone. I could feel her love and strength supporting me when I wasn't sure I could bear the pain any longer. I could hear her whispers that despite my medical prognosis, I would improve. I believe my work and worship of Macha has been a pivotal part of my healing. I still have more progress to make. I have doctors who would like to take credit for my medical miracles, but that honor goes to Macha. She inspires me to refuse the stifling gag of toxic patriarchy perpetuated into modern medicine where women's voices lose credibility and control of our care is stolen from us. When preparing for another doctor's appointment or procedure is the equivalent of preparing for battle, worshiping a Warrior Goddess empowers healing and self-advocacy.

Dark Lady
Words and Art by Kat Shaw

I am The Dark Lady.
I stand in the Shadows.
I sit with you in Sadness. Desolation. Hopelessness.
I hold you in your grief.
I am the Goddess of The Veil, The Unknown and The Dark Forest.
I am your anxiety that you cannot put your finger on.
I am the incompleteness that you cannot explain.
I am the nagging internal voices. The critic. The terror.
I am your fear when you encounter the unknown.
I walk beside the biggest unknown – death.
I will not lure and coax you back to joy.
Instead, I will lay down next to your broken soul.
You are never alone.

Yet I am also your sense of joy. Relief. Release.
The ecstasy of overcoming your obstacles and terrors.
The reflection of your shadow who now decides to befriend you.
I will walk with you in the darkness.
I will be your companion as you journey from fearful to fearless.

I am the Goddess of the forgotten in society.
I seek the lost and the unseen. Those shunned. Unwanted.
Those who do not fit in.
Those who are forced to dwell on the sidelines.
Those with mental health issues, who carry trauma of any kind.
Those who are bereaved. Those who have lost.
Those who carry shame. Those who do not fit in their bodies.
Those who are afraid of how and who they love.
Those who have been beaten. Those who have buried secrets.
Those who strive kindness. But never find it.
The homeless. The sex workers. The drug addicts. The abused.
I am the Goddess of mistreated and caged animals.
Who suffer at the hands of evil. Who have no free will.
Whose souls have been imprisoned behind bars.

See me next to you. Walking your path with compassion.

184

My rams horns show you your true strength.
Feel my wings as I enfold and embrace you, they fill all of time and space.
Dark as the night.
I can hold the sadness of the world.
For I was born with so much hope.
And I too have been knocked down.
My smaller wings show the devastations of life.
The tears, the breaks, the imperfections.
They are vulnerable. Paper thin. Easily broken.
Yet they remain.
For you.
They bear the weight of the sadness and troubled emotions that I carry.
For you – my people. And my animals.
My forgotten souls.

I am fierce and forgiving, with a love and loyalty so strong.

My silver skin holds the scars.
The lines of scar-tissued flesh that I have taken.
Through love, from you.
To ease your suffering.
To limit your pain.
To wipe your slate clean.
To transform you.
And I rise, silver and radiant.

I am pure compassion and empathy.
I emanate love from my shimmering heart.
I am stealth – still as a shadow.
Always there.
I will seek you in your most desperate and darkest moments.
And I will wait.
Wait.
Wait.

Until you are ready to walk into the light.
Because you are worthy of the light.

I love you.

How Patriarchy Perpetuates Trauma

M^h

What Women have been experiencing for millennia is no joke, no coincidence, and is the most silenced reality on this planet. This, the greatest secret, is one of the most painful truths to realize. To wake up from a nightmare within a nightmare.

What psycho-spirituality calls awakening is an event, or series of events, that tortures a mind and soul in such a deep and incomprehensible manner that the out-of-body aftermath leaves an individual either completely destroyed, or to pick up the pieces – most of which have never been recognized prior, with a newfound force. And then, to wake up and finally see things from a new lens that sees everything so clearly – to never be unseen again. The last blow that impassions you to furiously recognize all the strikes that came before.

What I, and many Women, call awakening is a feminist awakening. A consciousness raising – as torturous, enlightening, relieving, and enraging as any other, if not more. Our herstory. Something you cannot unsee, as you cry tears for yourself and all your mothers before for the occupation, rape, and murder of Woman. Of life.

The Exile: Separation from Self

It starts when you leave your body.

In *Wildfire*, Sonia Johnson told the story of her bath time with a girl cousin as a child.[19] As her aunt supervised the washing, the girls were informed not to touch their genitals but splash water on them instead as these parts were for their husbands. "My husband at the time was about five years old and living in

_____
19 *Wildfire, Igniting the She/Volution*, Sonia Johnson, Wildfire books 1989.

187

Wisconsin. I'm sure he had no interest whatsoever in the fact that he owned some little girl's reproductive organs in Utah. But I can remember the feeling that experience gave me about my relationship with my body, and I can best describe it as house sitting until the landlord comes home." She wrote.

While we may not all have experiences as clear and out in the open as these, most of us are taught from a young age to disconnect from, neglect, and starve our filthy, sinful, promiscuous, and gluttonous bodies. Our horrible flesh. Sentenced to become exiled minds wondering lost and desperate for connection, grounding, and wholeness – as buried as this pain, resentment and longing may be. We are abandoned, ready for anyone else to come make a home out of a deserted plot.

And to add to the blow, if I am to be completely honest, it really starts when your mother, who has for years been out of her body, cannot connect and expects you to do the same. You look in her eyes, but no one is home.

Of course, we are not allowed to say this, or speak of this next type of severing...

Separation from communities of individual Women

As we grow and learn that we will only come alive when our landlord arrives – when we leave father's world and enter that of our new master whom we have been searching for as we have only one goal in life – we learn another deeply painful lie. We have enemies on this journey. These enemies look like us.

There is real meaning behind the concept Divide and Conquer. We are bodiless, homeless, and we have no one to turn to. We are hurt by sistas and sisters who look like us – harmed by dethroned queens. As we look at the ones who deny us the support we desperately need, lie to us, betray us, stab us, do not trust us, as we feel the same towards them, we see ourselves. We are wounded by ourselves and what was once a community. It is a double and suffocating rejection. These unique reflections who have been scapegoated by the enemy that tells us we are enemies.

In the 'best' of circumstances we are allowed to only disrespectfully smile politely at each other and engage in a superficial, non-consequential relating as we make it clear our main focus is on other things and these banal 'real-life' commitments are all we have in common.

The white-supremacist, patriarchal males have never really had to put much effort into harming and de-lifing us or even do it directly themselves. Instead, they get us to do it for them.

These lost unique reflections. You look in her eyes where once lived a Goddess, but no one is home.

So, you continue to wait for your landlord.

And come he does.

The Occupation Disassociation

It starts with disbelief.

The men who are supposed to love and protect you are not acting as though they do. He says he does, but you cannot feel it. When you timidly mention this, you are the wrong one. You are the irrational one. The demanding and ungrateful one.

You are protected but it feels like stifling suffocation. 'Loved' but you aren't allowed to love yourself (neither is anyone else). You are granted leeways but you have to ask. This process itself is a soft dagger to the spirited soul. The loss of agency kills another piece of you. You bodilessly embody more powerlessness.

And this is only if you're lucky. If your oppression and repression is arbitrary alone. Sometimes you're not. He says he loves you, but the abuse is blatant. He says it's a free world, but you and your people are starving. He says you can do it too, but you have to try so much harder, and you will be scrutinized along the way. He says you can orgasm, but the focus is making him cum, and you have to do it and you have to do it in one way.

Of course, you haven't learnt names for any of these things. You don't even believe them yet. You are in denial. Having already been groomed and desensitized, this limbo state is only expounded by the betrayal, confusion and threat that is too much for you to presently process if you cannot escape – this system ensures that nobody can – and so naturally you disassociate. It is basic survival. This is the one instinct that still allows you to look a little human. Again, no one has to try very much; your essence is now giving in.

Trauma-bonding

It builds up with the trauma bond.

Now you can tell that something is *very* wrong. At least you intuit it with your sixth and seventh senses. But you still have some will of life, of source. You must survive.

We live in a world where, be it in mass media, in conversation, you hear phrases such as 'it hurts so bad it's good.' 'love the way you lie,' 'beauty is pain.' The joy of the mother who has just experienced the most pain of her life after giving birth is constantly used (positively of course) as a biblical metaphor for honor in suffering in the Christian religion as well as many other patriarchal ideologies. Mass pornification celebrates the brutalization of Women who allege themselves to be happy 'sluts,' 'whores,' 'bitches' and punching bags who LOVE to be BUST wide open and TAKE IT like the cunts we are. It would take too long to look deeply at all the language itself. But we don't have to. We just have to look at Women's lives.

It doesn't feel so bad it's good.

It feels so bad I must pretend to myself it feels good to survive this horror I can't escape.

To make my oppressor happy. To not offend them. To not be murdered. To embrace the confusion that I've been nurtured in. To balance the terror, shock, and pain with feelings of excitement, love and a desire to get closer. To be okay.

This trauma bonding involves many other means:

Reversals

Many of the above can be included here. Pain is pleasure. Women are not to be trusted. Women love and get off on the torture of Women. White men are oppressed. Women caused the fall of **man**kind. Bodies are death. God created the world (by some incomprehensible, biological miracle).

Gaslighting

Gaslighting is a combination of all the tactics of confusion and self-doubt that keep women trauma-bonded to patriarchy.

In the film *Gaslight*,[20] Paula's husband Gregory Anton employs a series of tactics that causes her to question her reality and sanity. One such instance is him switching the lights on and off in the

---

20 *Gaslight*, 1944 film, based on Gas Light, 1938 play, Patrick Hamilton.

attic. He tells Paula she is imagining it all when she questions the flickering.

All Women have been gaslit.

'That hurts.'
'You're too sensitive.'
'I want more,'
'You're needy/unrealistic.'
'I never said/promised this I said...'
'I don't remember...'

And so, you begin to think, maybe nothing is wrong but me, maybe I am too sensitive, maybe I am naïve, maybe this lifeless reality is life and there is something wrong with me if I am not fulfilled. And so, YOU begin apologizing. No one has to do much else. Ever wonder why Women are always sorry? Sorry for being crazy. Just sorry for existing.

When it comes to Women, *no one* remembers anything. And this is why everything continues. Another piece of your soul is lost. You're more dependent on and vulnerable to the offerings available.

Silencing

It ends with silencing (or speaking up and reclaiming our home + land).

I have never been someone to call *anything* something other than exactly what it is. This is a real threat to patriarchy's fragile ego. For so long Women could not even see **who** patriarchy is and is benefiting, and for the most part still can't.

We are not allowed to say it. Nor do we know what it is. There are many of these unnamed 'its' in Women's lives and herstory.

Again, this silencing employs many tactics:

Invalidation

Someone who knows who they are cannot give away their own selves, their own home, their own power. Let alone a Woman. Everyone sees Women's worth but Women. This is not a mistake or misunderstanding.

Women are the embodiment of self-love, and so we are stripped of this and given internalized oppression instead.

Women **know** things, see things, feel things, sense, intuit. Women use common sense and direct experience, an innate Goddess spirituality. Where Goddess is here, Goddess is within us, and Goddess **is** us and all of natural life. We are stripped of all of this and given a transcendental god somewhere out THERE. Every Woman learns this.

Women know we are Creatrix, Destroyers, Healers – the foundation of this EaRtH that is our inheritance. We are stripped of this intrinsic identity (at least mentally) and cast as the side-characters.

The Inability to Name our Pain

We cannot heal from what doesn't exist.

FORGIVENESS – 'honour' + 'righteousness'

This has been a very difficult one to grasp. I have experienced this difficulty personally.

As a human-Woman who stands for humanity, I have never accepted the concept of forgiveness – the *idea* that someone can 'forgive' someone, and someone can 'wrong' another. As grown adults that is. I have seen forgiveness be the opposite of love.

And yet who in our society does this and recommends this kind of forgiving? And yet who in society **DOES** get wronged again and again and must forgive – not in the petty self-righteous/entitled but most heavily dishonorable way – but out of outer (other) 'honour' and 'righteousness.'

These values come from an elusive male god that benefits the boys club and appropriates Creatrix/Goddess/Ma and her SPIRITUALITY (that is denigrated to moral 'religion.')

When I hit an epiphany about this horrific form of silencing called forgiveness, I started to come across various experiences about the HIStory and creators of forgiveness. I came across one video that brought it all together and sealed it for me. A video by OlaOmi Amoloku entitled *Forgiveness Dishonors Your Humanity*.[21]

This offering revealed the oppressive/judaeo-christian purpose of forgiveness—who is supposed to be forgiven (looked up to and given power over too) and who is supposed to forgive (look up at their oppressor from their lowly, unnatural and inhumane state that says it's okay you can treat me like shit you are still worthy I am the one who is not.)

I look at all the other fake patriarchal 'spiritualities' and even non-spiritual dogma that perpetuate 'forgiveness type' feelings and notions. I have long questioned the positivist – *it's all in your head, life is what you make it right now* – (another Creatrix appropriation turned around) agendas.

Basically, our history doesn't exist, our future is not important. But why? Because what has been done to us? What will continue to

---

21 *Forgiveness Dishonors Your Humanity*, Iyalosa OlaOmi Amoloku, Got2BOshun YouTube channel

be done to us? What will happen if we remember these things and organize ourselves for our future? We stop the alienation and silence.

We are in charge of our reality; we are the reason things are going wrong for us. *Why?* – So, we can stop holding accountable the people charging at us with knives.

Forgiveness doesn't exist. Your pain does – The harm that was done to you does.

Your anger exists. Your trauma is real and screaming to be catered to. As the video mentioned previously tells us – you can heal, we can move on – but you cannot and must not think you can or should forgive. The body does not forget. This is how we survive and heal.

Silencing is the end of everything.

Some final notes as I lay all this out for us and explore how we can heal and how Goddess-spirituality actually allows this healing.

An insidious form of abuse that has come to the surface over recent years has been called Narcissistic abuse. This abuse entails idealization, isolation, triangulation, gaslighting and finally devaluation. A Vampiric parasite dead inside preys on and sucks the sap out of life-embodying, empathetic and nurturing persons. It is hard not to find the parallels here with patriarchy and the constant trauma of Women. Systems that live, grow and thrive off of our Goddess gynergy are being exploited and expropriated – man-made systems that attempt to tame and take from nature – unsustainable systems with no life of their own that constantly need more and will continue to need more. Goddess is drained, Goddess fills herself back up, and Goddess is lied to, idealized, used, shamed and drained again.

I have used much language of land and colonization. Firstly, because unlike our father who art in heaven, our Ma is right here on EaRtH embodied in us. She is me, she is you, she is nature, she is immanent, real, reachable, all of us and all of life experiencing itself. She is the Woman who has come before and the Woman coming after me.

But mostly because the nature of patriarchal trauma and its appropriation is not separate from any other oppression and rape/theft. This is another secret. The secret that the first human who walked this EaRtH was a coloured Woman. Goddess encountered in human form to enjoy EaRtH. Both have been stolen, robbed of life and made into a ridiculous joke.

The reclamation is total and is no metaphor.

And finally, I am not looking to the 'experts', and I did not rely on them or anyone outside of myself and the assisted clarity of the Goddesses mentioned to create and write this offering. I will end with another statement from fellow Goddess OlaOmi Amoloku.

"I am not telling you what I think, I am not telling you what I've researched, I'm telling you what I know and what I have lived."

The Seed Blessing

Sue Ellen Parkinson

Healing from Patriarchy's Trauma Perpetuation
M^h

The Re-cla(i)m-ation

Separation from self

It is time to come home, Goddess. It is time to sit on your throne again or for the first time in this life. It is time to see yourself, to see your own reflection, and meet a full, living, breathing, joyous human being there. Meet the Woman you needed in your mother's eyes. Meet the Goddess you needed in your loving, supportive friend's (existent or non-existent) eyes.

Some suggestions for coming back to self:

- Mirror work
- Sensual self-exploration of your entire body
- Re-defining and re-living your sexuality
- Eating what you want and what you need
- Journaling
- Creating
- Picking up a long given up hobby once again, or finding a new one
- Talking to yourself
- Writing yourself an honest and revealing apology letter (the only person you can 'forgive' is yourself for forgiving trauma)

Separation from communities of individual Women

Let us take the time (out of our own genuine free will and inner guidance) to apologize to the sisters we have misunderstood, hurt, and left out in the cold – whether or not they hear our remorse. Let us take the time to empathize with ourselves and with these other Goddesses. And let us seek out brilliant new Woman play friends every day – Woman to spin and weave with; Women whose minds we explore and bodies and essence we enjoy; Women to banter with and laugh with; to indulge in the sin of pleasure and true passion with; Women we appreciate, deeply. Women we honor. Women we respect. Women we cherish. Women we need. Women who need us.

Disassociation

Becoming re-associated with ourselves involves coming back into our senses, into our experiences, into our very real bodies that have experienced very real trauma and very real joy. The many practical elements we can try to involve in this process are the same as those we could explore when returning to our Goddess selves; this is essentially the same experience.

Suggested exercises/reading for re-connecting with our traumatized bodies (and the bodies we came from):

- *What is the Mother Wound?* by Bethany Webster
- *Trauma and the Unbound Body: The Healing Power of Fundamental Consciousness* by Judith Blackstone
- *The Body Remembers* by Babette Rothschild

Reversals + The inability to Name our pain

Silencing is the end of everything.

Subservience and subversion are two very closely related words, as with everything in patriarchy's mind-fucking system. The opposite of **internal** and **external** silence is clarity, discernment, deep soul-searching, and yelling from the strongest vibrations of our fifth chakra, everything we fucking find there.

And just as importantly, moving hand-in-hand with this is re-creating our own language and naming patterns and using these expressions in the creation of our own narratives. Mary Daly, whom we will soon honor, has left behind an incredible Creatrix spark and pool of offerings for us to begin exploring.

Gaslighting + Invalidation

One difficult task we're pushed to learn as Women in this giant and personal patriarchal system is to validate our own experiences and emotions. Nobody taught us this, and we are pushed to learn it because nobody will teach us. It is this or obsessively seeking external validation that never suffices or hits the spot quite right.

The same way we have been soothing others, we must learn to soothe ourselves. The same way we have been affirming others, we must affirm ourselves. Because sometimes the closure does not come – and in many cases never will – we must give ourselves closure. In this portion of the task where we must walk alone, we really must do it ourselves for ourselves.

As much as genuine support is what we need and what has been stolen from us, this idea of crippling, helpless, infantile overdependence is also an intentional patriarchal scheme. We are far more powerful than we have believed ourselves to be. Our resources and inner strength run so much deeper. We can surprise ourselves, and often do find ourselves in such situations where we do. I don't need daddy, I don't need mommy, I don't need boyfriend/girlfriend/falsefriend for this. I am a grown Goddess. This is my task.

And only when I am rooted in this sense of inherent worth and 'I'm going to be okay I can live this,' can I be sure that the people I have pre-selected and **do** reach out to truly know who I am; a self-respecting human-Woman – and I can reaffirm this for me when I'm led to forget.

Listen to the voice of Goddess within as she asks you these questions:

'What if what I think is correct? What if I remember things correctly? What if my intensity is only 'intense' in waters too shallow for my soul? What if I am right, and the other person is right, and we can agree to experience things differently without me desperately losing myself by considering and fearing these natural differences as abandonment or shaming? What if I am the only expert on all things me? What if other people are the only experts on all things them?'

In times when I know who I am, I know what love is, and I know who loves me, it helps to make an ICE (In Case of Emergency) list of the people I will call if I ever forget these things and need the reminder as anybody needs water to live.

Reaching out will always be important in the desperate moments our herstorical experiences inevitably drive us to, I only want to stress the importance of the right support, that I must know myself and my passion for my life to even be able to identify who else knows me too.

Trauma-bonding + Internalization/ Narcissist-Empath dance

I will begin with the most powerful option whenever it is available (safe), if even for a short while: space, separation, no contact.

As homeless (or 'unoccupied') Women many of us have learned to submerge and drown ourselves in the waters of another, to merge to the point of self-annihilation to soothe this very same annihilation. We do not understand ourselves, the things **we** do have little effect—and in actuality, even our own bodies, states and perceptions are vicarious reactions to some other, and we must always see everything (including ourselves) through another's eyes. The danger presents itself when no one is home in those eyes either. The danger arises when those eyes have their **own** body and own intentions.

Let Goddess only ask of you to ponder all these things: That we cannot 'fix' anything or anyone else let alone all the messes we anxiously see; that we must come face to face with our very own co-dependency; that we cannot be blamed for our abuse, but it does take two to tango and certainly to continue the dance; that providing everything for somebody else will not satiate our own hunger and thirst; that external compasses and robotic religious respect do not have our best interest at heart and get us nowhere; and that patriarchy cannot perpetuate the fight against Goddesses who have put down their swords and walked away to create and restore their own worlds elsewhere.

(Very limited) List of real-life (past and present) Goddesses to assist us, to honour, and to thank for their offerings on this Journey

Maya Angelou
Audre Lorde
Sonia Johnson
Valerie Solanas
Sheila Jeffreys
Andrea Dworkin
Mary Daly
Kate Millett
Phyllis Chesler
Judith Butler
Peggy Kornegger

Sue Monk Kidd
Alicia Keys   YOU
Paris Warner
Iyalosa OlaOmi Amoloku
Willow Smith
Bethany Webster
Trista Hendren

We need to hear the Names of fellow Goddesses as well as our own Names over and over again. As many times as they have been silenced and hidden and more.

Again, these are not *expert* opinions but lived, tried, and tested suggestions.

The Flood

Liz Darling

The Flood (Triptych), center photo.
Watercolor, Gouache, Gold Leaf, Collage, Colored Pencil, Marker, Image
Transfers and India Ink, 2020

Who Am I?

M^h

I am Goddess
I reside in the very depths of Your soul

I am Goddess
I am the Trees and their Leaves and the Bees

I am Goddess
I am both the Tides that are pulled and the Moon that pulls

I am Goddess
I am HERe on EaRtH

I am Goddess
I am all things Bodily

I am Goddess
I am ever real

Some call me godless
But I am Goddess

I am Your lived experience
I am Your late-night conversations and moments of connection
I am Your intimacy
I am Your smiles
I am Your joy
I am Your tears that refuse to tolerate torture
I am the spark
I am the fire
And I put it out

I am the elements
The sun that touches, loves, and soothes You
The water that nourishes Your body and gives Her life
The air that You breathe in connection
the thoughts You think for Yourself
The soil that You walk on the soil You have tasted
when beaten down on my grounds
My grounds that I have gifted You

Who am I?
I am Goddess

Some call me godless
But I am Goddess

Night and day You can call out to me,
Though You really need not even whisper
My radiance is within it would be difficult to miss her

For I am Goddess
I am You

The Seed

Arna Baartz

Embracing the Divine Feminine: How the Patriarchy Perpetuates Trauma (and How to Heal from It)

Dr. Denise Renye

We live in a society that devalues the feminine (aka, yin, shakti, etc.) energy – meaning the one that creates space, turns inward, and is powerful in its receptivity. We could also call it Goddess energy. Marion Woodman says, "The Goddess is the unspeakable wisdom that grows into the very cells of the body. She lives with this sacramental truth at her center: The beauty and the horror of the whole of life are blazing in Her love. She is dancing in the flames."

The Goddess has been all but banished from our fast-paced, patriarchal society. Even though she can be a fierce force of nurturance, she is very different than the cut-throat attitude of everyday capitalistic values that govern most of the world.

We see this lack of care mirrored in the ways in which we speak to ourselves. Think of how people use harsh self-talk in order to get themselves to "have willpower" and stop overeating, go to the gym, earn more income, climb the corporate ladder, etc. The commonplace ways in which we speak to ourselves is toxic masculine and it goes beyond the voices in our heads – it's also how we speak to women, nonbinary folx, and anyone who is on the more feminine end of the gender spectrum. We tell them to "speak up" in meetings, to lean in, to assert themselves, otherwise they run the risk of being bulldozed. But why should that be the case? Why is it that we encourage men and people on that end of the continuum to take up space and to be heard whereas women have been taught to be "listeners" and "space holders?" A consensual listener is very different than a forced one. Yes, the loving Goddess is receptive and understanding, but she's also firm with her boundaries while being caring about psychological as well as physical safety. But how we treat women[22] is not with safety in mind. We see this in something as simple as how frequently women interrupt each other, which is approximately 2.8 times during a three-minute conversation (Robb 2014).

It's clear some women have internalized misogyny and sexism, which can be experienced as the likelihood to put other women down, sabotage their successes, compete with, and disregard other women or girls' identity, contributions, and successes. These are all at least somewhat familiar to most women as they have become commonplace in society. In fact, the patriarchy thrives when women are pitted against each other. All of this equates to patriarchal trauma.

Patriarchal trauma is the complex, multifold injury – psychological, social, emotional, spiritual, financial, and physical – associated with living under patriarchy, understood as the oppression and denigration of all things feminine that do not directly or indirectly cater to the traditional masculine. Patriarchal trauma is any and all ways women, feminine expression and understanding, and the prioritization of relationality are told they're "less than," not allowed to be, or exist visibly in this world even! Fear, judgment, belittling, and downright violence constitutes patriarchal trauma. This sort of trauma permeates the fibers of most societies around the globe and is the foundational aspect of capitalism and the corporate world.

And even the concept of winning creates a binary. There's a winner and there's a loser. That itself is a concept that splits people apart and keeps parts of ourselves from relating with other parts of ourselves. I know, it seems like the cis-gendered White man is the reigning champion and "wins" under patriarchy, but he

___

22 Please note, when I say "women" I also mean nonbinary folx and people on the feminine end of the spectrum but it's too cumbersome to write that every time.

does not. Patriarchal trauma affects everyone across the gender/sex continuum – self-identified men and women – because men cannot truly be themselves, especially if that means being caring, vulnerable, and soft individuals. Furthermore, traditional society continues to not know how to handle or what to even do with transfolx. This is a disservice to all, and it serves to uphold the patriarchy as it is.

Not being allowed to be yourself is a form of trauma. Trauma is also abuse of the sexual, physical, verbal, or emotional kind. There are more kinds of trauma that are not related to patriarchy, but/and for the purposes of this essay, think of it as any experience that overwhelms your nervous system and ability to cope. It can leave you feeling helpless or enraged, so yes, dealing with a patriarchal system counts.

What happens when a person is traumatized? The "self" can split off into different fragments, leading to dissociation. Psychologist and philosopher Dr. Eugene Gendlin (2007) sums this up nicely when he wrote:

"What is split off, not felt, remains the same. When it is felt, it changes. Most people don't know this! They think that by not permitting the feeling of their negative ways they make themselves good. On the contrary, that keeps these negatives static, the same from year to year. A few moments of feeling it in your body allows it to change. If there is in you something bad or sick or unsound, let it inwardly be and breathe. That's the only way it can evolve and change into the form it needs."

However, many people have not been taught to "inwardly be and breathe" as Gendlin suggests. Instead, people often cope with trauma in self-sabotaging and self-medicating ways such as with alcohol, other drugs, or excessive eating/exercising/restricting and body hatred to name a few. They may not even realize they're reacting to trauma and instead just trying to feel better from the immense overwhelm that is flooding their system. A fish doesn't know it is in water, it just exists. A person with trauma doesn't know they are in a hellscape, they just are. Are we doomed to keep living in the hellscape known as the patriarchy? We certainly are not but in order to evolve beyond it, we must embrace more feminine ways of being. That is the way to move beyond it and the way we can mitigate the effects of patriarchal trauma despite continuing to endure it.

To heal requires bringing in the body no matter how much some mental health professionals continue to try to neglect it. Trauma is *not* only stored in the brain as a memory (like was previously thought), but instead is stored in the body at a cellular level. That means just as the mind and body registers an event (or events) as traumatic, the mind and body can also release those traumatic events. As a psychologist, here are some techniques I've found are helpful for releasing trauma from the body:

- Somatically oriented depth psychotherapy
- Massage therapy
- Body movement (dance, sports, yoga, shaking, etc.)
- Hugging
- Non-performative art
- Laughing
- Crying
- Breathing
- Chanting or singing
- Free-write journaling
- Drumming
- EMDR
- Psychedelic-assisted therapy and integration
- EFT (emotional freedom technique)

Anything that puts you back in touch with the body and helps you feel safe will be nourishing for your body and mind. Also, healing from trauma involves support and feeling safe in the presence of someone else. That could be with a friend or partner, or it could be with a trained professional such as myself, but not in a way that retraumatizes you through regurgitation of the event(s) over and over again, rather in a way that helps you process it and release it, such as through somatic-oriented depth psychotherapy. The body and mind must be honored and addressed simultaneously.

Addressing through the mind, traditionally overvalued by the patriarchy, is not enough. The body, traditionally undervalued by the patriarchy, must be included and at the forefront of this healing process. The overlooking of the body is the overlooking of the feminine. It is the overlooking of the ancient ways of healing that have been more Goddess-based and earth-based. Our bodies are of the earth.

As you release trauma from your body, note that your body can also start acting of its own accord. For instance, it might do any of the following:

- Shake or tremble
- Change in temperature (i.e., sweat or get goosebumps)
- Cry
- Yawn
- Clench the muscles
- Collapse the muscles
- Fidget and express other nervous movements

These are all normal reactions so do not be alarmed! It is natural for our bodies to begin to seemingly have a mind of their own. I also use an exercise with my patients to invite them to slow down. I may say to them: "Could you notice your breath?" If they're still feeling distraught while noticing their breath, I say: "Can you bring your attention of your body to the couch (or chair) and all the points where your body is in contact with the couch (or chair)?"

This tool of noticing provides a space for being in the present moment.

If the breath or heartbeat can be identified somatically, I may say: "Would you stay with that and see what else arises?" They might say something like, "My chest feels tight." I'd ask them to use their breath and bring attention to whatever is tight and breathe right into and through the tight spot. I check in with them after they've done so and ask them what they notice now. This technique draws from Gendlin's work on something he coined as "Focusing," a way to work with the bodily felt sense and the living process.

They might say they feel at ease or expansive. I would invite them to expand that sense of ease or expansiveness out to a few inches beyond their body, or a few feet. I'd invite them to expand it out to the size of the room, to the size of the building, the size of the block, inviting them to take up more space energetically. Taking up space is something that typically diminishes as someone is working through an initial traumatic event or a retraumatization.

Then I might say: "I invite you to remember that the sense of expansiveness is something you can continuously come back to because it exists within you." Healing is an inside job. I am merely a facilitator of helping people to realize their own healing potential.

I work with people via depth psychotherapy, coursework, and coaching programs to not only heal, but also assist them in meeting the Goddess in a form they might be ready or open to meeting Her. She may come in the form of a comfortable new chair to replace an older one that's falling apart. She could show up in earth-based activities such as hiking or communing with plants. She might even be the fierce, loving voice encouraging a person to cut off a toxic relationship for good. As for me, an avenue I use frequently personally and with clients is the walking meditation tool, the labyrinth.

The labyrinth is an intentionally created design to engender a lived experience; it may or may not be affiliated with any religion or sect. The labyrinth is a metaphor for life. You pause, take a break, charge forward, become annoyed if someone is "in your way," or even experience loneliness if you are walking alone. Alternatively, you may feel a sense of solace being alone. There's one way in and one way out, but along the way there are many twists and turns. There are no dead ends, no wrong choices like in a maze. Instead, there's an understanding if you keep going, eventually you will reach the center of the labyrinth. And you just might find the Goddess was with you the whole time, walking at your side.

References

Gendlin, E., 2007. *Focusing*. New York: Bantam Books.

Robb, Alice. "Women Get Interrupted More – Even By Other Women." *The New Republic*. May 14, 2014. https://newrepublic.com/article/117757/gender-language-differences-women-get-interrupted-more

Tree of Life

Rebekah Myers

I heard my Mother call to me
and went out
into the greenwood.
I heard her voice
in the whispering
of the leaves.
Up, I looked
into the green-roof;
shadows and light
mingling together.
I saw my Mother's face
smiling down upon me and knelt,
her arms encircling me,
holding me close.
I felt her strength flow
into my hurt places,
mending my brokenness;
healing my woundedness.
I lay for a time between firm roots
and felt the burning in my flesh
cooled; eased.
I rose, able to return to the house
and carry on.
I will not forget my Mother,
who came to me there
in the greenwood,
within the tree of life.

Wet Spring

Liz Darling

Watercolor, India Ink, and Gouache
2019

The Awakening of the Goddess
and the Healing of Patriarchal Trauma
Rev. Christian Ortiz, Ph.D.

We live in a time of confrontation of great truths, where the spiritual and the political converge from the individual and collective conscience. The flourishing of the Goddess movement in the 1970s brought the opportunity to do a spiritual and social rereading of the power of women and the sacred feminine in patriarchal culture. The Goddess reemerged as an archetype, political symbol, and spiritual force in the world. In the 21st century we can claim the denied power of the Goddess; she has never stopped walking in the world, she is the world.

She has been hidden, chained, denied, trafficked, and nullified; but the indomitable spirit is much greater than any oppressive or colonizing system. Just like women and everything "feminine", she cannot be devastated. She continually returns, she has always been like this and will always be this way. She is the truth and the temple below the temple.

The systematic war against women is real, the persecution and the inquisition have changed forms, but essentially it is the same. Its malicious objective has been to "tame" women and, if not succeeded, destroy them. Survivors are transformed into monsters or are erased from history. The spiritual power of the Goddess cannot be erased.

The Goddess has used so many names and garments, but even in this time she is still seen by most as a simple myth (not in the real sense of the word, but as a lie or children's tale), something evil and destructive, or a simple metaphorical speech. She touches the mythical, the artistic, the religious, the social, etc. She is in all those spaces, no category limits her, she is unlimited.

What we have done to women and to the earth, we have done to the Goddess. Our only way of integrating her in her right place will not be by raising temples and re-creating liturgies; her power will be manifested in the freedom of the bodies and souls of girls, women, and everything we call feminine.

We are called to return to the Goddess in her multiple cultural and religious manifestations, her symbols are spiritual bridges to create new ways of relating to the body, the earth, and others. It is useless to create altars to the Goddess if we despise and hurt women and life itself, we are the temple.

The uncomfortable truths have come out to light and today we can affirm that the exploitation of women and girls, the exploitation of the land and the ecological (and cultural) devastation to sustain the elite at the top is real; so far away from HER, so disconnected, so lost, so close to extinction.

Patriarchal trauma and chains of pain

Patriarchal trauma includes various levels of suffering that are being addressed by different disciplines. However, its impact is real and manifests itself on the level of cultural, psychological, emotional, spiritual, and physical well-being or discomfort.

This complex and collective trauma causes transgenerational pain, driving systemic pathologies and imbalance of power between the genders.

Under patriarchy, boys, men, and "the masculine" are considered inherently superior, while girls, women, and the feminine are considered inferior. The extreme social positionality of superior versus inferior causes distance between the genders and distorts the possibility of a truly healthy connection between the "genders". These genders are a created cultural reductionism that denies other forms of existence, also causing binary heterosexism;

a premise that dictates heterosexuality as *woman – feminine* and *man – masculine* as the only valid categories of existence.

All families are affected to a greater or lesser extent by gender violence and only some are in the process of healing. The patriarchal trauma affects all areas of life, and impacts each individual differently, depending on their position in their culture.

Under patriarchy all people are trapped in pain and violence; women, girls and Mother Nature are the main victims. Men and masculine beings are trained as unconscious machines for the generation of violence and pain. This occurs, through the *mindset – programming* of hegemonic masculinity, causing internal and external pain. We are all part of the cycle of repeated pain like a continuous echo, a cry of suffering that is passed from generation to generation.

Returning to the Goddess, as a metaphor, spiritual center, archetype, model of connection, philosophy, religion, or way of life is urgently needed to begin the work of healing and liberation from patriarchal trauma. Returning to the interconnection matrix is an arduous process; it is not frivolity or nonsense. The Goddess continues to manifest herself more and more; either due to an intuitive need of the human species to survive, or as a conscious phenomenon resulting from the understanding of the traumatic imbalance that we are experiencing.

Artists, priestesses, activists, politicians, etc., from the four directions of the world raise their voices to awaken the Goddess in the souls of all people. The Goddess has returned and with her, the possibility of a peaceful, loving, interconnected and equitable world.

Breaking the chains of pain is a multidimensional healing process that requires personal and collective effort. It is very difficult to heal if we do not have a diagnosis; we cannot heal a wound if we do not know where it is in our Being.

Within patriarchal trauma as a complex and collective phenomenon, the following are included:

- Transgenerational - intergenerational trauma
- Racial - cultural trauma
- Religious - spiritual trauma
- Family trauma
- Body trauma - sexual
- Other dimensions of personal and collective trauma, suffering and pain

In all the previous traumas the patriarchal mentality is manifested as the cause of suffering, guilt, and shame. We can heal through the Goddess and her strength, she is MOTHER WORLD, the one who is beyond judgments, the one who grants understanding, dignity, tenderness, and liberation.

MOTHER WORLD is a metaphor, spiritual force – archetypal to speak of the indestructible force that inhabits the spirit of creation, therefore, also within us. She is the one who breaks the chains and has manifested with multiple faces of feminine divinities. She is Mother World, Mother Love, Lady of mercy, Mother of rage, Breaker of chains, Protector of the helpless, Force of life, etc.

All trauma healing requires an understanding of the damage suffered, a narrative that explains what happened to us. It is also necessary to know that other worlds are possible, inside and outside of us, that we are not alone and that we are not guilty of the enormous chains of pain. The Goddess is a spiritual force with multiple cultural narratives of dignity and empowerment that gives us the possibility to walk in the world again with love, understanding, compassion, and dignity. She is in us and we in her sacred body.

Patriarchal trauma must be resolved collectively and personally. Some points are:

- Prevention and attention to violence
- Protection of children and women
- Education for peace, especially in beings socialized as men
- Recovery of care and self-care as a center of social connection
- Expression of tenderness and intimacy
- Recovery of the mind / culture matrix and the power of the maternal
- Cultivation of collaborative relationships and overcoming dominance-submission relationships
- High sensitivity and re-sacralization of the land
- Peace-making revolution and the principle of no war
- Eco-sustainable cooperation
- Constructive and non-supremacist rationality
- Eradication of the instrumentalization of sentient beings
- Multicultural valuation and rupture of nationalist identity

These points are some proposals that I make, based on a polarization of the principles of the patriarchal mind of the beloved and admired Claudio Naranjo, psychiatrist and specialist in human integration processes.

The patriarchal mind is a concept coined by Claudio Naranjo in 2010. Through this concept he intends to explain the culture of industrial and post-industrial society in which true reason dominates the senses and destroys the weakest and nature, since it is seen as something given to human beings, as something that can be thought in mathematical terms, hence in today's societies the exacerbated cult of reason and technology prevails.

Its mysteries to heal collective trauma

The great truths cannot be the monopoly of anyone, throughout history, multiple cultures, traditions and religions have observed deep truths, they are present in the perennial wisdom. Goddess hides in her metaphors, legends, rites, cults, and other human manifestations. She is the mystery behind the mysteries, she is the ANIMA MUNDI, our sacred mother, the voice of the earth.

I share some mysteries kept in simple truths. Our Sacred Mother is always in the obvious, she is Nature.

Sacred garden mystery

The mystery of life is gynecological, we are part of a fruitful garden where nothing is bigger and nothing is smaller. The unhealthy hierarchy is part of the patriarchal culture, it denies Goddess and turns us towards the exploitation of the earth and other beings. In an ecosystem, every being is of vital importance for the maintenance of balance. In Goddess we are all important and sacred, her spirit reveals this to us through the natural laws of life support.

Sacred cobweb mystery

She is the great spider woman who weaves and weaves reality, in her divine web everything exists and is interconnected. When we understand her mysteries beyond the mind, beyond speeches, we will never be alone again. She is a weaver, we live, die and are reborn in the sacred fabric.

Cradle and grave mystery

She is not a sugarcoated stereotype of kindness, tenderness, and compassion. Those are just stereotypes of the feminine, and they have been reinforced to oppress women. Her nature is beautiful, she is the great transformer. In her bosom death is life, life is death. Our bodies and spirits are on a continuous journey of integration and disintegration, there are no endings, only doors that close, while others open. She is the mystery of eternal life that mutates and acquires new clothes.

Moon and sea mystery

Nature endows us with mobility and cyclicality, not even the dead stay still. There is a universe of cycles that even in what seems dead, is in continuous movement. The moon and the cyclical nature of the sea bring us closer to the dancing mystery of the world. We live in a beautiful dance that operates in many dimensions. No one can get out of its influence and rhythm. If we learn to enjoy her sacred movement, our lives will be more fruitful and blessed, if we don't we will create suffering. The spiritual ego driven by patriarchal traditions makes us believe that the divinity is punishing or rewarding us as little beings in training. The world is much more complex and beautiful than that narcissistic and childish vision in which we were raised. It's not about earning divine favors; it's about syncing up with its rhythm.

Names mystery

She is not limited to a space/time; therefore, no figure, symbol or name encloses the totality of her. From an interreligious and cross-cultural vision, we understand that the divine cannot be enclosed in a single human manifestation. She appears from diversity, is colorful and variable like nature. Her names and forms are bridges for our human understanding. We create affinity according to our cultural and personal characteristics and deep needs. If we understand this, we will stop discriminating and trying to change the spiritual and cultural code of other people. There are blonde Goddesses, brown Goddesses, red Goddesses, yellow Goddesses, black Goddesses and they are all beautiful. They are beautiful because they are a reflection of her children.

No one should be mistreated and discriminated against if we understand the mystery of their names, which is why they have so many. She is a spiritual, political, psychological, and cultural reminder of the value of diversity.

I want to remind you of some of her names:

Mami Wata reminds you of the power of black and beautiful. The dignity of the African diaspora and her love, that transcended along with her sons and daughters. They couldn't destroy her holy presence. Her skin color is black, and she is beautiful. No one else should ever hurt her loved ones. Mami Wata, the great transatlantic slave voyage did not extinguish your flame, you live in our hearts!

Diana reminds you of the great power of women together. She walks in feminist marches and goes against rapists and aggressors. They cannot destroy the power of the circle. She unites and sustains them with love and strength for all. Diana, you live in our hearts!

Coatlicue reminds you of the indomitable spirit that cannot be killed. She has risen with her titanic strength and has said NO to the conqueror. Is the temple below the temple. She is reborn and emerges from the earth with the memories of people, she is a link with our past and dignity. Never again feel ashamed for being brown, never again kneel before the aggressor. Mother Coatlicue lives in our hearts!

Kwan Yin reminds you of the healing power of compassion. She washes your wounds and makes you look at the scars with self-love and compassion. She says stop the toxic critic inside and outside of you. You are not guilty of everything that happens. The world is a better place when compassionate tears cleanse our wounded view of the world. Kwan Yin is in our hearts!

The Goddess and her multiple names, colors, shapes, and voices are in our hearts... and in the world!

She is always calling us, she does not live in a single tradition, in a single temple, even less in a book. Her sacred book is the silent manifesto of nature and her rhythms, her prayers are the fair and dignified treatment for all her creations.

Our Goddess-centered spirituality is part of a complex and beautiful movement that can be the prelude to planetary change. Our mother calls us into her arms, our lady claims her power, our Goddess is in the world!

With love and respect to my sisters, mothers, classmates, and teachers. To the Goddess, the one who lives in the eyes of all women and girls.

May we return to MOTHER WORLD.

Take it Back

Caroline Selles

Warm waves of delight
Shudders of joy
The Universe inside me, glorious
Complete, profound
I know this place
I have been here before
Long ago, when life was magical
When summer nights meant chasing
Fireflies in the dark
When summer days meant feeling
The cool of the grass as you rolled down the hill
In ecstasy
Childhood is where you learn to be free
If you survive it
Become like the child who was
Unaware of shame
Unaware of danger
Unaware of sin
Like a child, know only sounds
Textures, temperatures, colors
Freedom
You should be free
Free to know your own body
Free to roll down hills of joy
Chasing fireflies

Wild Flower (Vagina & Child)

Caroline Selles

The Goddess in the Garden:
Ode to My Divine Anger

Ellie Lieberman

It was said she was from the sky and the earth. Her name was spoken in hushed whispers for only the chorus of crickets to hear. I was not supposed to know her, but I did. I knew her like I knew me. At least, like I knew me when I was younger. When I was not so separate from the trees and the wind.

I came to her when the moon was full, and my belly swelled with centuries' worth of burning that was becoming significantly harder to swallow. Nails bitten to the quick dug marks into my palms and my lips were bloody and raw from being snagged one time too many between clenched teeth.

I needed an escape, to flee for just a moment. Just a moment where the building pressure could ease like a long-tight fist, finally beginning to relax. A moment where I didn't need to look over my shoulder. Hold my breath.

I fell to my knees in the grassy field. The sky gradually darkened above with the first shine of stars emerging from the cloudy haze of gray. As my eyes lifted, I shivered at the wind wrapping around me like a shawl. It made pinpricks along the back of my neck, an intuitiveness often mocked and dismissed.

I was not alone.

When I fervently searched the growing darkness, all I could see were the shadows I was always taught to fear. Yet, I could sense a presence.

"If you come to me, come to me on your feet," the wind whispered, smelling sweet, like roses and jasmine. The voice was tangible, as though if I were to reach out my hand, my fingers would feel the sting of some sharp, invisible thorn.

Hugging myself, I rose. Suddenly, I feared the wind would turn cold and distant. A fleeting thing until I'd be left with nothing but this burning.

A snake slithered around my feet, hissing a laugh of delight as I danced around her, startled. In the blink of an eye, the creature stood upright on two feet. A cloak of shadows replaced scales. The hood hung low, obscuring her face. Only a pair of painted, red lips could be seen.

Her smile unfurled like a datura flower in the moonlight. The seeds it could plant would be just as dangerous.

Instantly, I had questions tickling the tip of my tongue, as though this being were a reflection of me. Questions I'd never dare ask outside the darkness and solitude. Forbidden questions. Like stolen cookies before dinner.

What knowing lay beneath my bone-deep stirrings? The scars that spread their tendrils across my flesh and heart? Am I more than the echo of my own breathing, trying to calm the war-drum in my chest?

She reached up and plucked a pomegranate from a tree. As she split it open, the juices dripped, staining her hand red. She tossed half to me, scooping up the seeds and stuffing a handful in her mouth. She licked her fingers one by one, well aware of my eyes on her. She was hungry, unapologetic, and she seemed to only grow by the seconds. Towering and haunting and beautiful in her wholeness, her muchness.

I looked down, tentatively slipping a seed between my own lips.

She had questions of her own. "Why do you feel the need to shrink yourself, become less than what you are?" Her voice was a tree-branch scratching, owl-screeching wolf-howl. It fed the fury and flames still lapping in my belly.

"Do your ghosts leave you?" I spat, but my eyes remained downcast. She smirked, but it was less amusement or condescension and more respect at the challenge.

"Which ghosts?" she hummed. With a wave of her hand, a spiderweb sparkled with memories. "Don't look away," she warned. "Don't turn away." My feet rooted in place as her words became a thread, tying me to her and the web. I could not take my eyes off the days of my past and her past and memories that were not mine, that I'd have no way of knowing. Every woman before me and after me, playing out in moonlit dew reflections and reverberations.

"Your grandmothers hid it in their perfect lace and stitched it in each embroidery. Their carefully cultivated garden. Baked in every pie. A spell to remember when they once flew with the birds overhead and dove into the mysteries of the ocean-depths. When they were armed with swords and wit and silver-tipped, diamond-cut spells dripped from their tongues. They thought we were tamed. We were merely a stone, carved by the whipping, unforgiving wind and sharp river waves, but still standing strong."

"Can you feel it?" she whispered. "Your great-grandmother held you below her heart when your mother was but a gleam in your grandmother's eye. You carry more than her name."

"Be it whisper or windstorm," she went on, "you survived. You live between the lines, reclaiming the roots they tore from the ground and the wings they clipped. Surviving the best way you know how."

"Who told you big wasn't beautiful?" She took a step closer to me.

 "Who told you loud was a sin?" And another. "Who made you feel like a stranger in your own skin?" And another. "Who broke you, then called the mosaic you pieced back together ugly?" Until we were nose to nose and I could feel her fire, bright and brilliant and wild, feeding my own. The questions were rhetorical. She knew.

 "Who taught you to fear your own divine muchness, fullness, wholeness?"

Anger is dangerous. Too often, it's been a weapon in someone else's hands and called righteous, powerful, justified. Too often, it's been suppressed in me and my sisters and mothers, called over-sensitive and hysterical. I never met a woman who wasn't angry, and they've all had reason enough, whether scorching on the surface or smoldering buried deep. But, the parasite was never the anger itself.

"Aren't you supposed to be the answer?" I snap.

She threw her head back and laughed, heartily, knowing the risks of playing with someone else's fire. "I'm an outstretched hand, the spiderweb. I walk beside you, nothing more." She offered her hand, waiting.

"Taste the ash. Stoke the coals. Wrap yourself in the smoke. Dance with the flame and come to know it as you know me, as you knew yourself when you were young. Burn bright and fearsome. For you are not a china doll. You cannot and could never be tamed." She howled, head still turned up toward the moon, soaking in her brilliance and shine. "Anger is divinity."

I took her hand, warm in mine, and together we danced. As dawn broke, my anger, my fire, had yet to extinguish but, for the first time in a long time, I felt at home. The war drum in my chest raged on, but the knot in my stomach was a long-tensed fist finally relaxing.

Her cloak stretched out, like wings. As she spun, she took the darkness with her. Feathers replaced fingers and, in the blink of an eye, a raven, big and regal, rose into the foggy gray sky, leaving behind a trail of smoke.

Joyous Body/Universe

Alissa DeLaFuente

Burdensome Dance

C. Abigail Pingree

Agree to all the possibilities,
agree to fly or fall,
to sink, swim or sail.
Say yes to them all,
because before you lie your fate,
be it miraculous or fierce,
probably both...
As the bird sings its evening song at twilight
so must you sing, then take your rest,
then arise again tomorrow and greet the day.
This burdensome dance,
be willing, be willing.

Remembering Goddess Through the Motherline: Healing the Patriarchal Wound

Rita Shahi

The Goddess path is a deeply personal commitment for female spiritual development. This path is a journey that requires traversing psyche with internal reflection, self-exploration, and introspection. Laden with joy-filled heart openings, auspicious synchronicities, and glorious Aha! moments, the unfolding process also leads to experiences of emotional upheavals, inner turmoils, and lucid encounters with the soul. Like the Goddess herself, the process is circumambulatory. For healing to occur, one must peel through layers of inner psychic terrain to seek wholeness. As emergent qualities arise, Goddess gently but firmly reaches her hand out and leads the way down a winding road of self-discovery. This spiraling path descends into realms within psyche that require mulling, tending, and weeding to unblock hidden parts of the self. Perera (1981) suggests that to heal psychological wounds of the shadow, descent is a necessary process and that, for women, this includes sifting through cultural repressive aspects of patriarchy.

The motherline and patriarchy present a cobweb of psychological disruption that many women face. Within the current patriarchal model, cultural emphasis is placed on patrilineage. This obscures, erases, and veils the sacred feminine experience that lives and dwells inside each woman. The split with the Great Mother Goddess relates to the psychic model of women's disconnect within themselves. The split from Her reflectively mirrors a way for one to peer into their soul for reconnection to happen.

This fragmentation of what was originally known as a whole symbol system is also reflected in our psyches. Psychologically, the process of reaching the completed Great Goddess means first feeling our own fragmentation, and dropping down through the many overlays of collective patriarchal constructs (Reis, 1995, pp. 54-55).

In a quest to move through patriarchal cultural and personal wounds, I explored my motherline heritage through the lens of goddess spirituality and Jungian depth psychological techniques. I took a journey toward healing the past in order to move forward.

Who Am I?

For over two decades I have walked with Goddess. I am a priestess in Her service as a healer, guide, and ritual facilitator. To be a priestess is to know who you are and from where you come. The call to re-remember the Goddess through my mother lineage came shortly after my mother's death. I felt an immense void. When I lost her, I lost part of myself.

I found my way to graduate school in the Depth Psychology department at Sonoma State University. Here, I delved deeply into Jungian psychology working with conscious and unconscious aspects of psyche. My explorations of the self, led me to connect with my Croatian roots, the Goddess and my motherline. This propelled a profound journey to unravel intergenerational patriarchal traumas. My curiosity to dive deep into ancestral roots of who I am and where I come from guided me to a deeper connection with Goddess and healing. I examined what patriarchy has to do with personal and cultural wounding within my Slavic motherline. I used a Jungian technique called *active imagination,* a liminal lucid dreamlike space that engages a series of dialogues with imagery that present to psyche the power of creative imagination (Johnson, 1986; Jung, 1964). This sparked an internal awakening that spontaneously led me into a distant past back in time a long time ago. Here, I heard the call to come Home....

The Ancestral Call HOME

Dead silence looms as the atmosphere is dry, except for soft quiet whispers of the wind brushing up against my face. I look over the hills, the valley, and into the trees. In the far distance, I see Crna Gora, "Black Mountain," it is Montenegro from which my ancestors came. I hear the cries of my ancestors perched atop this mountain, "Why have you left us?" "Where are you?" "Where have you been?" The subtle whispers begin to grow louder, "It is time," "It is time," "It is time." "It is time to remember who you are and where you come from." I listen. From the inner depths of my being, I turn inward with visions flashing before me as the story unfolds, and I retreat far back in time. In my imagination, I come across a time of being intricately connected to land, trees, birds, and sea. A time and a place where reverence for all life is honored. I hear the cries of my ancestresses, they want to be known, they wish to reconnect me to this place and so it is, that I come. It is time now to remember where I come from. It is time to re-remember the sacred feminine through my motherline.

A Journey Home to My Motherland

I embarked on a pilgrimage to the Old Country, Montenegro, the land of my maternal heritage, in the summer of 2017. I came by way of Croatia to deepen my sense of Slavic culture and from whence my ancestors migrated hundreds of years ago. On my drive from Dubrovnik to Montenegro, I bore witness to physical and emotional Slavic cultural wounds. I sat for hours in the car with the glaring sun beating down listening to my driver tell stories of war and the role of the Church.

Wounds from my ancestral past were cut open as my driver, Antone, expressed anger and hurt over the loss of his friends, his own loss of self, and his internal battle of rage and hostility toward the bloodshed of war that he experienced in the 1990's. He blasted the control the Church currently has on his country. He referred to his mental breakdown as an "interruption of the head." The blood of the horrible Serbo-Croatian wars left Antone institutionalized and in the hospital for several years. Being here in the land of the Balkans defined the dis-connect clearly. The term "to balkanize" means to divide and compartmentalize hostile smaller regions into groups. It was evident that the scars of this bloody war were still freshly etched within the soil and fabric of these people. I pondered over thoughts of my own matrilineal lineage and the traumas of endless wars. I reflected upon the women, the generations of women particularly, along my matrilineal line and what they endured from the repercussions of the wars past. Anderson (2015) writes, "Grandmother of 1912 would become the outline for Grandmother 1994" (p. 5). My female ancestral lineage undoubtedly felt and experienced similar pangs and oppressions from war. Many generations of my ancestors were affected of living in a war torn region that was not of their own making.

The effects of transgenerational transmission of trauma and the recent physical mother loss I experienced triggered me to explore a deeper wound within myself. Jung (1965) states that the ancestors and the land of the dead appear when there is soul-loss. He further postulates that loss can happen when a disconnect from the ancestral past occurs.

The Self and the Dark Goddess

I turned to the archetype of the dark goddess. Myths of the goddess offer a timeless existence through the ages and mirror an inner and outer reality that assists in unveiling shadow material. In Inanna's descent myth, Ereshkigal, the dark goddess, is heard moaning in the Underworld. These moans of being cast in the Underworld reflect the culture of the time when the social status of women began to lose power (Perera, 1981). These moans are ultimately moans of feminine loss. My moans challenged me to drop into the depths to face shadow material, and I met the archetype of Ereshkigal as my projected self.

My dreams were profound. I followed their thread. I fell into the despair of loss. The loss of culture, family, and the loss of my mother. I felt into patriarchal fears of self-worth and value and the tight reigns of control the Church had on my family and my formative years. While on my stay in the ancestral village of my grandparents, I had the following dream titled *Church Blood*.

> *I see an image that moves across a screen of rust colored blood smeared in front of my eyes. I hear a distant echo. The ancestor calls for me and says this blood is associated with the Church. The female voice then directs me to the roots of a lineage through imagery. She is a guide.*

Lowinsky (2009) states that to embrace rejected parts of self means looking at and acknowledging the mother and her lineage. I witnessed my soul gripped in a continuous generational mode of patriarchal constraints. The stiff sense of fears within myself is perhaps the same felt sense that may also have been generationally experienced by the women in my motherline. There is no doubt that war and patriarchal rule create dis-connect. Power-over leads to oppression and suffering at their hands. I found solace in making connections between self and the ancestral past by returning to my motherland to mend female generational wounds. Following the thread of ancestral connection allowed for healing to happen.

Healing and Transformation of the Sacred Feminine

The lucid dream-like dialogue, *The Ancestral Call,* was a precursor to the psychic road map that eventually led me in direct contact to the mother-daughter goddess statues that stand proudly atop Lovçen. When I embarked upon the journey to Montenegro, I had no conscious realization what I would stumble upon. I had no idea

239

that Lovçen existed or that it was literally Crna Gora, the Black Mountain, the exact mountain envisioned in my active imagination. It was pure happenstance that I encountered Lovçen at all. A series of mishaps with my daily itinerary left me at an impasse and circumstances out of my control led me to what appeared to be a popular destination site. What I didn't know was that I was led by greater forces other than myself.

Arriving at the base of the mountain, I ascended a long and very exhaustive climb entailing 461 stars that seemingly appeared to lead to infinity. I felt a resonance with this place and felt that I was being divinely guided. An awareness gripped me that this pilgrimage happened for a reason. I came to realize that Lovçen had been calling me all along. I didn't know anything about what stood upon this structure; only that I had made it to the highest peak in Crna Gora. I walked a short distance on the flatly paved walkway when my eyes suddenly came into focus upon something just ahead. Two humongous statuette figures visually revealed themselves the closer I came to approaching them. These two gigantic figurines stood as pillars on either side of a gold framed mausoleum. The figures were two goddesses, mother and daughter. It was as though Demeter and Persepone were there to greet me. It was then that I realized the Goddess and my ancestresses directly led me to Lovčen.

The two female statuettes atop Crna Gora signaled the cultural implications of what had once been prior to the patriarchy, and the value and equanimity of woman. Perera (1981) contends that there is an internal hunger for the feminine to relate to symbolic images that depict the feminine mystery as a relatable model to help engage a woman toward wholeness. These striking figurines pose as personal and cultural icons. They signify a return to the spiritual matriarchal center and the return of the feminine as a sacred healing source that is necessary to attain wholeness.

I didn't realize the impact visiting Lovçen would have. My active imagination, *The Ancestral Call,* a year and a half prior, and the constellating energy of holding this image, directed me exactly to this particular mountain to heal ancestral wounds. This was an affirmation of the healing power that the Goddess path offers and the depth practices I used to circumambulate back to her. She carried me through stages of a psychological growth pattern that cumulated back around to my initial beginnings and my search to re-remember the sacred feminine within my motherline.

Remembering Goddess

The day before my departure I was given one last reminder of Her presence within my life. Strolling along the cement sidewalk along the glorious inlet Bay of Kotor, I stopped short at one of the vendor booths where my eyes caught the attention of ancient goddess figurines. These actual pieces on display had been excavated from the Vinča archaeological site in Belgrade dating back to the Neolithic period (Gimbutas, 1971, 1974). First, I held the Bird Goddess in my hands. One by one I held each of the goddesses feeling the antiquity of an ancient past. The two other small statuettes were Demeter and Aphrodite. I cherished these significant gifts handed to me from my beloved motherland. I felt them to be offerings not only from the Mother I synchronistically encountered on Mt. Lovçen but also gifts from my ancestresses who originally cried out from the mountaintop to come Home. According to Gimbutas (1989), the Bird Goddess represents the guardian of the family and oversees the continuity of life and the well-being of its members. I viewed these statues as farewell gifts for making this pilgrimage, as a way of not forgetting Her and my maternal ethnic roots. The statues would be a lasting reminder of a re-remembrance of this sacred healing journey I so tenderly and wildly embarked upon. I no longer felt a gaping hole in my heart from the loss of my mother and the motherland she never knew. She was there guiding my heart all along. These Goddess treasures travelled home with me as a re-remembrance from whence I came. My circle, my *kolo,* felt complete... Her cycle ever so continuous.

As mothers, daughters, and granddaughters, familial wounds get passed down generationally. Effects of war and acts of violence carry highly transmittable effects for generations. Healing from ancestral patriarchal wounds is a journey, unique and varied for every person. The goddess and her myths aid to connect the thread of ancestral roots by offering meaningful ways to glimpse into the past, inform the present, and heal fragmentary splits within the psyche. Exploring our inner psychic terrain through depth techniques such as dreams and active imagination often leads to meaningful encounters with the Goddess who lives and dwells within each woman. My sincerest hope is that in sharing this personal account back to Home will foster an enriched sense of Self for women who search to heal patriarchal wounds as a quest toward wholeness. My hope is that this spiritual road map aids women to dive deeper into themselves, their motherline, and Goddess as a path to transform wounds and reclaim that which is our sacred birthright.

References

Anderson, D. (2015). *Blood and Honey: The Secret Herstory of Women: South Slavic Women's Experiences in a Modern Day Territorial Warfare.* Olympia, WA: Kolo Press.

Gimbutas, M. (1971). *The Slavs.* London, GB: Thames & Hudson.

Gimbutas, M. (1974). *The Gods and Goddesses of Old Europe: 7000-3500 BC, Myths, Legends, and Cult Images.* London, GB: Thames & Hudson.

Gimbutas, M. (1989). *The Language of the Goddess.* San Francisco, CA: Harper & Row.

Johnson, R. A. (1986). *Inner Work: Using Dreams & Active Imagination for Personal Growth.* New York, NY: HarperSanFrancisco.

Jung, C. G. (1964). *Man and his Symbols.* Garden City, NY: Doubleday & Company Inc.

Jung, C. G. (1965). *Memories, dreams, reflections.* New York, NY: Vintage.

Lowinsky, N. R. (2009). *The Motherline: Every Woman's Journey to Find her Female Roots.*

Cheyenne, WY: Fisher King Press.

Perera, S. B. (1981). *Descent to the Goddess: A Way of Initiation for Women.* Toronto, Canada: Inner City Books.

Reis, P. (1995). *Through the Goddess: A Woman's Way of Healing.* New York, NY: Continuum.

The Healing Circle

Sue Ellen Parkinson

Can I Climb on Your Lap, Mama?

Sharon Smith

I hurt.
Everywhere.
Can I climb on your lap
And rest my head against your ample breast?

I need you, Mama.
To hold me.
To tell me it's going to be okay.
To soothe me
And make the fear and anxiety go away.

I feel lost, Mama.
Nowhere to turn.
In a world where your Daughters are

Beaten,
Battered,
Mocked,
Scorned,
Overworked,
Underpaid,

Called "Nasty Women"
Sluts
Whores
Bitches,
Witches.

And are
Used,
Abused,
Raped,

Murdered,
Missing,
Forgotten.

Can I climb on your lap, Mama?

~~~~~~~~~~~~~~~~~~~~~~~

My Beloved Daughter,
I hear your cry,
I feel your pain and sorrow,
And I want you to know:

I am here for you, always.

Yes, yes, come onto my lap
I shall hold you close to my heart;
I shall rock you gently in my arms
And let you rest.
And I shall tell you a story...
But it may not be the one you wish to hear.

I will not lie to you, Beloved,
I cannot tell you everything will be all right,
Nor will I say the world will not be cruel to you.

But I will tell you this:

You are Powerful.
You are Strong,
You are Beautiful,
Intelligent,
Brave,
Resilient,
Resourceful,
Persistent,

Imaginative,
Creative.

You are Wise.
You hold within you
Pearls of Great Price
That no Man can steal away.

You have
A Song to sing,
A Story to tell,
A Poem to write,
An Image to paint,
A Thought to think
A World to create.

I shall comfort you, my Sweet One,
But I shall not coddle you.
I shall wipe the tears from your eyes,
But I shall not promise there will be no more tears.

Life is not meant to be easy;
It is meant to be lived—

Through the good times and the bad times:
As Summer yields to Winter,
So, too, your life will have
Seasons of Warmth and Cold,
Moments of Light and Darkness,
Times of Fertility and Barrenness.

But I am here for you,
To Teach you and to Guide you,
To remind you of Who You Are
When the lights go out,

So that you will not despair
To walk where you cannot see.

And if you fall, my Beloved Daughter,
I will help you to your feet.
But you must dust yourself off
And keep moving forward.

Because that Path you're on?
It's yours.
And you must walk it on your own.
But do not fear, my Darling,
You can do it!
As long as you remember this:
You are stronger than you think!

Say it over and over again to yourself!

~~~~~~~~~~~~~~~~~~~~~~~~~~~~~~~~~~~~~~

Yes, Mama, I hear You.
Thank you, Dear, Wise Mama!
I will say those words.
I will say them until I believe them:

I am stronger than I think.
I am stronger than I think.

I AM STRONGER than I think...

[Note: This poem illustrates how the Goddess, our Great Mother, helps
us through trauma and difficulties—not by coddling us and protecting us
from diverse troubles, but by comforting and encouraging us to
remember who we are, and that we have a Sovereign Self who is
Powerful and Capable to meet and overcome any hardships that
confront us along the way.]

She Came from the Stars

Arlene Bailey

Hidden Gifts

Maureen Owen

I believe "stories can change the world".[23] For "what we believe, to whom we belong, how we behave and who we become are profoundly shaped by our stories and the larger narratives in which we live".[24] Hidden gifts can be contained in stories and often appear when you least expect. Last year I received such a gift when a friend spoke of having "the courage to walk into our own story and own it". The idea of this struck a chord so deep it sent me on a quest to do just that. This story is of what I discovered.

The quest has not been as straightforward as I first thought. I've learnt that it involves reaching within and reaching back as much as it requires reaching forward. I've found that this is also about "survivorship, healing, and thriving"[25] and becoming.

It's also a story about secrets. Secrets like those held by many women, heroic dramas that at first glance seem to be tragedies that go nowhere.[26] Nonetheless, just below the surface I've found an undercurrent, a part of the story not usually revealed. And it's this part that contains the "the knife of insight, the flame of the passionate life", the breath to speak what one knows, the courage needed to stand what one sees without looking away, and "the fragrance of the wild soul".[27]

---

23 Rebecca Solnit, *Recollections of My Non-Existence*, 2021, p244.

24 David Drake, *Narrative Coaching: Bringing Our New Stories to Life*, 2015, p310.

25 Clarissa Pinkola Estés, Ph.D. *Women Who Run with The Wolves – Contacting the Power of the Wild Woman*, 1993, p197.

26 Clarissa Pinkola Estés, Ph.D. *Women Who Run with The Wolves – Contacting the Power of the Wild Woman*, 1993, p376.

27 Clarissa Pinkola Estés, Ph.D. *Women Who Run with The Wolves – Contacting the Power of the Wild Woman*, 1993, p21.

The knife of insight

The day the knife of insight first fell, all hell broke loose. I was sixteen years old, and a terrible ruckus arose from the house across the street. There was yelling, and in the yelling was a very discernible sound of a woman screaming and of a man yelling obscenities in response to her cries.

There was also the sound of things smashing. We rushed to see what was transpiring for we were not used to such goings on, or at least that's what I thought. To our horror, we found the man across the street dragging his wife by her hair. Her face bruised, her clothes torn, her screams and cries filling the air.

The police came and I returned to the house, where I found my beautiful and kind mother, cowered in a corner weeping and shaking. I thought of my mother as someone who could handle absolutely anything. So, her response seemed disproportionate to what we had just witnessed. I asked her what was wrong. Was there something else troubling her?

It is in that moment I learnt that my mother had spent the first ten years of her life terrified of her father and his drunken rages. She told me that when he had been drinking, which was often, he would come home and take out his anger on everything and everyone. From the second the gate closed; they knew; for the yelling and obscenities would start.

First, he would take the horse whip to her brothers, then he would charge through the house breaking everything he could find. The more precious and more sentimental an object the more determined he was to destroy it. Her mother, to protect her and her sisters, would lock them in a bedroom. They would huddle together under a bed, terrified, listening to the yelling. This meant, of course, that her mother Rose would be subjected to the full force of the rage.

My mother's earliest memories were of being huddled under that bed listening to the destruction, listening to her beloved mother screaming for grandfather, Paddy, to stop. And then of Rose crying in pain from the beatings. On that day, many years ago, when I found my mother cowered in the corner, this is what she was responding to.

It is hard for any of us to live in a world where we feel in constant danger. It requires perpetual vigilance, a hypervigilance, a wariness worn at the level of the skin, and never being able to fully relax, never feeling completely safe.[28]

The undercurrent

The costs women and children bear in a patriarchal society where their worth is seen as being less than that of men[29] inflicts deep wounds that become imprinted on our psyche as women.[30] In spite of this wounding there is an indestructible soul-spirit[31] that once accessed will never submit to this oppression.

In my mother's case, she took the trauma of her childhood and determined to help other women and children. When I was growing up there was always room for anyone in need at our house. Women and children would suddenly appear. My mother would help in any way she could: with a place to stay; kind words; conversations long into the night; a meal here and there. All provided at a time when my mother, a widow with five children, struggled to make ends meet herself. From the millions of possible choices available my mother took the trauma of her childhood

---

28 Sarah Peyton, *Your Resonant Self, Guided Meditations and Exercises to Engage Your Brain's Capacity for Healing*, 2017 pp152-155 and pp198-199.
29 Valerie Rein, Ph.D. *Patriarchy Stress Disorder*, 2019, p131.
30 Valerie Rein, Ph.D. *Patriarchy Stress Disorder*, 2019, p131.
31 Clarissa Pinkola Estés, Ph.D. *Women Who Run with The Wolves – Contacting the Power of the Wild Woman*, 1993, p35.

and chose to create a new story for herself "of strength, resilience and empowerment".[32]

The same is true of my grandmother in the way she chose to navigate through the violence and abuse. A life where my grandfather's preferences for excessive amounts of alcohol, womanising, and gambling meant that Rose lived in extreme poverty constantly struggling to feed and protect her children and herself.

When she packed up her six small children and sought help from her own family, they sent her back, choosing to not believe what she was telling them. They thought she was exaggerating. The inevitable responses of "Rose surely not" and "Paddy would never do that" left Rose with no choice other than to return to the nightmare. The violence and abuse continued for what must have seemed like forever (which turned out to be another fifteen years).

Current research tells us that "often it is the experience of being ignored, dismissed, not believed, or told we were lying that" leaves the strongest mark.[33] The response of Rose's family to the most significant question of "does anyone believe, notice or care?"[34] must have left deep scars and a sense of utter despair. I often wonder how Rose survived, how she kept going, and how easy it would have been to descend into bitterness. Traumatised from her experiences she must have completely been "pissed off" with the broken promises, the broken marriage and her broken heart.[35] Yet stories abound of her as a strong and supportive

---

32 Albert DeSilver, *Writing as a Path to Awakening*, 2017, p135.
33 Carol Gilligan and David Richards, *Darkness Now Visible – Patriarchy's Resurgence and Feminist Resistance*, 2018, p128.
34 Sarah Peyton, *Your Resonant Self, Guided Meditations and Exercises to Engage Your Brain's Capacity for Healing*, 2017 p118.
35 Clarissa Pinkola Estés, Ph.D. *Women Who Run with The Wolves – Contacting the Power of the Wild Woman*, 1993, p364.

mother, of her kindness, her love of animals, her sharp wit, her intelligence, and her courage.

A favourite story that speaks to her strength of spirt, is a story that takes place one night when Paddy was away on business. She noticed a man lurking in the shadows. He was close enough for Rose to see him but not close enough to see who he was. She yelled "who are you and what do you want?" No response came back. She asked him to leave. He didn't budge. His presence growing more intimidating. She issued another warning . "If you don't leave, I'll shoot." He, of course, ignored her. So, as the story goes, she picked up the shot gun, loaded it, and took aim. His hat flew across the yard. He scurried away into the dark.

The next day stories ran riot through the town. Rose was being labelled a dangerous woman. The proof: a bullet hole in the accuser's hat. Rose was very proud of this story. Her favourite line, which she loved to repeat, was "she's a dangerous woman, she is, so she is".

Rose wore the badge of being a "dangerous woman" with pride. It seems that no matter how many times she was pushed down, somehow, she was able to bound up again, able to find the strength to continue. It is this strength that emanated from her and made her a force to be reckoned with.[36]

The flame of the passionate life

So where does this indestructible spirt come from? From the perspective of archetypal psychology and from traditions of storytelling, this indestructible spirit is the feminine soul.[37] The term feminine soul is "a woman's inner repository of the Divine

---

36 Clarissa Pinkola Estés, Ph.D. *Women Who Run with The Wolves – Contacting the Power of the Wild Woman*, 1993, p10.
37 Clarissa Pinkola Estés, Ph.D. *Women Who Run with The Wolves – Contacting the Power of the Wild Woman*, 1993, p13.

Feminine, her deep source, her natural instinct, guiding wisdom and power".[38] It is this indestructible soul-spirt I believe that was infused in both Rose and my mother.

This is not to say that my grandmother or mother would have used words like feminine soul or Divine Feminine. For they were deeply steeped in the Catholic faith. From this perspective women are viewed by the Church as naturally inferior, as the property of men, and associated with evil and sin.[39] Making terms like Divine Feminine appear as sinful.[40]

Yet what is striking, is both my mother and grandmother were deeply devoted to the Virgin Mary. And this devotion ran deep. When I was growing up, we would say the rosary (prayers dedicated to the Virgin Mary) as a daily ritual. When things were difficult, additional prayers were added asking for protection.[41] A practice my mother had learnt from her mother, and no doubt that Rose had learnt from hers.

I believe it is this devotion that enabled my mother and grandmother to grow stronger through these devastating experiences without becoming bitter. For whatever happened they had the Virgin Mary to turn to. Mary was a woman just like them, who as a human mother had "suffered every conceivable difficulty and drawback", there was no suffering or humiliation she herself had not endured.[42] They felt acknowledged and seen by Mary and thus able to access a feminine source of power that

---

38 Sue Monk Kidd, *The Dance of the Dissident Daughter – A Woman's Journey from Christian Tradition to the Sacred Feminine*, 1996, p20.
39 Sue Monk Kidd, *The Dance of the Dissident Daughter – A Woman's Journey from Christian Tradition to the Sacred Feminine*, 1996, p69.
40 Sue Monk Kidd, *The Dance of the Dissident Daughter – A Woman's Journey from Christian Tradition to the Sacred Feminine*, 1996, p72.
41 Alana Fairchild, *The Kuan Yin Transmission, Healing Guidance from Our Universal Mother*, 2019, p126.
42 Andrew Harvey, *The Return of the Mother*, 1995, p342.

didn't come from patriarchy or need to be validated by it.[43] Mary is a revolutionary figure who seeks social transformation, justice and love for humanity and it's this spirit that I see infused in them and their refusal to shrink and shrivel in the face of trauma and hardship.

The courage to stand what one sees

I am shocked and dismayed at how little this trauma has been spoken of in my family and at the intensity of wounding and neglect of the feminine. The level of abandonment, the amount of abuse and the suffering in these inherited wounds is horrifying and painful.

At the same time, I am revivified by the strength and presence of the Divine Feminine so deeply woven into the fabric of these women. This is a joyful revelation and immensely reassuring. The Divine Feminine has always been present and can be depended on in the most dire and dismal of circumstances. This is the source of the indestructible soul-spirt that emanates from the women in my family and the birthplace of their courage, determination, devotion, survival against the odds, and choosing of love as their response.

The fragrance of the wild soul

The fragrance of the indestructible wild soul, and its deep, deep roots are the hidden gifts unearthed on this quest. I have learnt that "gifts come in many guises"[44] and sometimes contain "equal parts pain and wisdom".[45]

---

43 Sue Monk Kidd, *The Dance of the Dissident Daughter – A Woman's Journey from Christian Tradition to the Sacred Feminine*, 1996, p75.
44 Rebecca Solnit, *Recollections of My Non-Existence*, 2021, p245.
45 Clarissa Pinkola Estés, Ph.D. *Women Who Run with The Wolves – Contacting the Power of the Wild Woman*, 1993, p198, p376.

The story that you and I are in "is much larger and longer than" just our own for we are all "in the gift of older stories we are only now joining".[46] I invite you to join me in strengthening the indestructible soul-spirit within on this quest of owning your own story and walking into it, and of owning our collective story as women as we walk into and claim that. For the wounds of the past will not heal until we own them and honour them with words and witness.[47]

It is time to move beyond merely surviving to healing and thriving. For "we were meant to dance and sing, play and laugh" and unselfconsciously tell stories, to "make love, and take delight in this brief but privileged adventure of incarnation".[48] For there "is no place so awake and alive as the edge of becoming".[49]

46 David Whyte, *Crossing the Unknown Sea – Work as a Pilgrimage of Identity*, 2002 p56.
47 Clarissa Pinkola Estés, Ph.D. *Women Who Run with The Wolves – Contacting the Power of the Wild Woman*, 1993, p377.
48 France Weller, *The Wild Edge of Sorrow*, 2015, pp51-52.
49 Sue Monk Kidd, *The Dance of the Dissident Daughter – Woman's Journey from Christian Tradition to the Sacred Feminine*, 1996, p12.

References

Brown, B. 2018, *Dare to Lead: Brave Work. Tough Conversations. Whole Hearts*, Vermillion, Penguin Random House, London, UK.

Beak, S. 2013, *Red Hot & Holy – A Heretic's Love Story*, Sounds True, Boulder, Colorado.

Campbell. J. 2013, *Goddesses, Mysteries of the Feminine Divine*, New World Library, Novato, California, USA.

David, S. 2016, *Emotional Agility – Get Unstuck, Embrace Change and Thrive in Work and Life*, Penguin Random House, London, UK.

Drake, D. 2015, *Narrative Coaching: Bringing Our New Stories to Life*, CNC Press, Petaluma, California, USA.

DeSilver, A.F. 2017, *Writing as a Path to Awakening,* Sounds True, Boulder, Colorado, USA.

Fairchild, A. 2019, *The Kuan Yin Transmission, Healing Guidance from Our Universal Mother*, Blue Angel Publishing, Glen Waverley Victoria, Australia.

Gilligan, C. 2003, *The Birth of Pleasure – A New Map of Love*, Vintage Books, New York, USA.

Gilligan, C. & Richards, D. 2018, *Darkness Now Visible – Patriarchy's Resurgence and Feminist Resistance,* Cambridge University Press, UK.

Harvey, A, 1995, *The Return of the Mother*, Jeremy P. Tarcher/Putnam, New Work, USA.

Kempton, S. 2013, *Awakening Shakti – The Transformative Power of the Goddesses of Yoga,* Sounds True, Boulder, Colorado, USA.

Monk Kidd, S. 1996, *The Dance of the Dissident Daughter – A Woman's Journey from Christian Tradition to the Sacred Feminine*, Harper Collins, New York, USA.

Peyton, S. 2017, *Your Resonant Self, Guided Meditations and Exercises to Engage Your Brain's Capacity for Healing*, 2W.W. Norton & Company, New York, USA.

Pinkola Estés, C. 1993, *Women Who Run with The Wolves – Contacting the Power of the Wild Woman*, Random House, London, UK.

Rein, V, 2019, *Patriarchy Stress Disorder – The Invisible Inner Barrier to Women's Happiness and Fulfillment,* Lioncrest Publishing, USA.

Solnit, R. 2021, *Recollections of My Non-Existence,* Granta Publications, London, UK.

Solnit, R. 2017, *The Mother of all Questions,* Haymarket Books, Chicago, Illinois, USA.

Weller. F, 2015, *The Wild Edge of Sorrow, Rituals of Renewal and the Sacred Work of Grief,* North Atlantic Books, Berkley California, USA.

Whyte, D. 2002,*Crossing the Unknown Sea – Work as a Pilgrimage of Identity,* Riverhead Books, New York, USA.

The Serpent Was Actually God

Alorah Welti

Wandering the hollow heart of the church,
she begins to speak.
Choked by the Bible pages in her mouth,
her frail tongue, a serpent.
Is this what Eve meant
when she said it would never be enough?

The coyotes sound their warning call,
laughing at her indecision.
She's been tearing at the veil of her faith for months.
Now the many multitudes of angels
try to spare her the grief,
"God hasn't been around much
since his mother died," they all whisper,
building her sonnets out of crow song
and their own black feathers of freedom.

When she is finally ready
I waste no time.
"*This* is what they don't want you to know:" I tell her.
"Spirituality is a feast.
There is no forbidden fruit,
you will not die.
You can take all you want."

I wait for her outside the church
and when she walks out,
her arms full
of apples, pomegranates, and sovereignty,
she is laughing and laughing.

Eve—Guided by Stars

Sue Ellen Parkinson

Sacred Call

Jen Abha

Moving through patriarchal trauma to truth, aided by Goddess, calls us to tap into her wellspring of compassion and grace, practice deep patience, and cultivate an unwavering insurmountable faith in her.

Prayer. Stillness. Communal ritual. Deep listening and devotional practices illuminate the light that is always stored deep within our wellspring of aspiring and aiming to return to her Truth.

Patiently, safely, arriving home, in the arms of divine grace, which enables us the strength and perseverance to overcome perceptions and limitations of the collective struggle.

Where we are met with beautiful reflections of our wholeness.

Our embodiment of healing is sensed internally, like a sentient ever-growing web of foundational support, with the open expansive heartfelt energies of all-knowing Truth. Our instincts are honed and refined as we get in touch with the wisdom of the ancestors who poured their full being, pregnant with Mama Gaia Earth energy, fused with an inner divinity that bonds our awareness and understanding of a matrifocal way of being, calling on our yin reservoir with the natural laws of alignment with elemental design atomized in wholeness.

Vital lifeforce charged with divinity.

Nature flows in me, around me, above, below, and all through me. She permeates the deepest layers of my beingness.

My divine spark of authenticity where the Truth coalesces into magnificence with the light of others, deeply committed to, and valuing the healing effervescent, heartfelt journey.
All feeling. All-knowing. Intuitive alignment.

The significance of Earthing. Aliveness through song, and dance. Play and imagination. Healthy movement. Structure and clarity. Uniting our voices. Cohesion. Nourishing earthfare found in local and organically grown fruits and vegetables. Fresh hydrating water to restore our energy bodies. Deep restoration and sleep. Human Growth Hormones. Nervous system regulation supports clear sight. Goddess aligns us to the laws of nature, which enhances our clear knowing. To walk our unique path, when we have the bravery to walk, and the faith to believe.

The communion of togetherness shared in purposeful and intentional rituals.

The never-ending, all supportive, all loving, all-knowing, benevolent circle.

The tools are here for us to call upon.

Radiating "I am"! "We are"!

The ritual that Goddesses bring forth to unite in sacred communion with our surroundings, the Land, one another, all living creatures to nurture connection to all elements of divinity.

To carve out, an intentional deep listening to all of life that resides in the domain that we share.

One planet • One people • One knowing.

Goddess calls forth my essence, with such clarity and dignity, that I no longer

Look away
Turn the other check
Are lulled into conformity
Am pacified into going along to get along

There is a <u>deep aversion</u> and <u>sheer unwillingness</u> to watch in silence and horror as the repeated patterns of abuse, misuse, neglect, and ignorance grip tightly on our progress of creating a future without Her vital and crucial imprint. 'ENOUGH!' Goddess ROARS.

Her healing tendrils of compassion spilling forth in all elements of our beings.

Sometimes quiet, and soft, sometimes ferocious and loud – weaving a healing tapestry:

I am Love.
We are Love!
And each one of us, always has been!

We are compelled to craft a purposeful, clear intention to unravel, unwind and unbind the unconscious control of the past and those unwilling to change their attempts to squelch our personal expression of sovereignty.

We know there is a different way. Of Being. With ourselves, and one another.

Yet, it requires Bravery. Courage. The willingness to transform and be transformed.

It is paramount we find the support. Internally, and as a collective to brave the belly of the beast. To change the ominous future that love will inherently and righteously be our legacy. As we reclaim the foundation from the past of that which were the bones of our Earth Mother. A love so deep and wide, long, and strong, a love that has never left, betrayed, or abandoned us and inhabits every fiber of our cellular matrix to build the scaffolding of a whole tomorrow.

Because the yesterday was insurmountable pain and separation. A pain so deep, it carved grooves of abuse, mistrust, hurt, betrayal that reverberates in the system until a brave soul in the circuit chooses to cease the ignorance and separation. And courageously accepts the call to embrace the aliveness of feeling and living fully. With clear objectivity and passionate visioning.

The grooves will continue to revisit us and inevitably the darkness will enfold and encircle us, with a desire to set into the known tracks. It is paramount we restore our connection to this heart centric work of returning to Goddess. With mindfulness and sensitivity. The like-minded soul cohort of connection. Take gentle care of your vulnerability when you are here, love. When you arrive in the dark, the dark offers you to love all of the places that you avoid in the daylight. The dark offers each one of us a moment to pause, breathe into the moments that may frighten us, cause us to feel afraid, constricted, incapable or unloved. To reconnect, and create a restoration to a way of being, thinking and feeling that calls us further inward to our home of self. The unwavering center that connects us to our own sacred, inner divinity.

From this place, we cultivate a gentle garden of love, more love than we have ever experienced before. We need to be loved in all of our shadows, and all of our light – in all of our phases and stages of our glorious evolution. We need to support ourselves as we do others when these moments arrive; continually giving us opportunities to enhance and grow, our inner and outer garden of love.

Answering the call to heal our ancestral roots and restore the safety of being alive on earth now, is an intense process. We are all being actively called to step forward and claim our Healing—to restore the soil on which we all walk.

Her connection, Her life-force, Her deep trust, Her honoring of our sacred yin vessel of deep, deep knowing, of life, eternity and universality.

Her connection to the Goddess of Mama Gaia and all of Her living beings.

The energy of our ancestral past where knowing is feeling, and living is being, is transmuted into a felt sense of beauty and aliveness, sensed in all dimensions of time and space, as together we worship Her sacred, all-knowing ways of healing.

With beauty.

With pleasure.

With lighthearted ease.

With Grace, and grateful hearts.

Our individuality ignites with passion as we see ourselves magnified in the Collective with a light so brilliant and wholly integrated, our aliveness overtakes any shadow of what once was, to bring to life a magnificent tapestry of healing, beauty, and fullness

Be still, my loves. Breathe.

And when the going gets tough ~
Have courage, dear hearts.

You were made for this work.

The sacred call visits you in the whisper of the wind, the stirrings of your imagination, your daydreams, the look on your loved ones' faces, the twinkle of the soul that just passed you by on the journey.

She calls to you, if only you feel into the beauty of Her.

I trust, each one of us will all awaken to Her magic and splendor. Our future depends on answering Her sacred call to awaken.

What a wondrous world we are co creating! Let's dream it and be it – each one of her Sacred Calls into vivid clear existence, to weave a tapestry of collective compassion and mutual togetherness.

May we all flourish, in service to our souls, and Her Collective. Will you join in the Movement?

Las Curanderas

Sue Ellen Parkinson

A Prayer to the GODDESS MAYARI
from the Tagalog and Kapampangan
Mythologies of the Philippines

Dona Tumacder-Esteban

Through this prayer, I invoke She who came to me amidst my battle with depression, the deep sleep of my creative Spirit, and the system that blinded me from healing deeply held trauma. It was Her who opened my eyes, inside and out. May she lend us her eyes to see our Selves into re-membering who we are.

I call on her, Mayari, the Warrior Goddess, the Goddess of the Moon, of Beauty and Strength, of Equality and Justice. I call on Mayari, the one with two different eyes, one eye seeing in and the other seeing out.

I call on her for courage to stand and fight for what is right when Apolaki, her brother, claimed sole leadership of the land after the supreme creator Bathala, passed without leaving an heir. She stood her ground and fought for her place as an equal and able co-leader.

In battle, she lost an eye. Upon seeing what he had done to his sister, Apolaki realized his rightful place, and, with deep remorse, apologized and offered shared leadership, him during the day, and her at night. I call on Mayari for her capacity to forgive Apolaki and accept his apology and peace offering without ill feelings, without retaliation. She took her rightful place and moved forward in peace.

May she grant us her two eyes for Clear Vision, one for the dark and one for the light. May she bestow upon us the Courage to stand our ground. May she endow us with Wisdom to know when it is time for war and when it is time for peace. May she fill us with the capacity for Forgiveness. May she bring balance to the Masculine and Feminine aspects within us so we can heal and live in Wholeness. And may she bequeath us with Strength to take leadership of our own lives, transmute our traumas, and be of service to the world, eyes wide open, one looking out, and one looking in.

Salamat. Siya Nawa. Bahala Na.

In the Beginning Was the Womb

Rebekah Myers

In the beginning
was the Womb.
In the Darkness
was the spark struck.
In the Consciousness of She
was the thought kindled.
With ruby blood,
with earth and bone
was the Mystery made flesh.

Oh, man, know
the secret women know.
Do not fear the source
of your own making.
Do not envy, nor deny,
nor re-write Her glory
into patriarchal story.

Womb is not witch
for you to burn.
Darkness is not evil
for you to dispel.
Mystery is not peril
for you to control.

She is the grail
of all your longing,
who from the beginning
went before.
Kneel,
Worship,
Adore.

The Empty Womb
Liz Darling

Mixed Media Collage on Bristol
2010

The Healing Power of the Closing of the Bones Ceremony

Rebekah Myers

Close my bones
Within the womb
Of my Mothers.
Knit my separation
Bind my brokenness
With ministering
With hands of love
Warm me
Within the dark peace
Within the womb
Of my Mothers.
Close my bones.
Make me whole.

The Closing of the Bones is an age-old ceremony practiced in Latin America, Morocco, and Indonesia by birth workers to give a postpartum mother healing closure both in her physical self and in her spiritual and emotional self after pregnancy, labor, and delivery.

It involves warming bone broths and herbal teas, gentle massage, bathing of the feet, and blessing.

The recipient is given a special massage using the "rebozo" or "manta" scarves to adjust and realign the bones and structure of the body. They are then bound upon vital points of the body and blessed with healing hands for full closure and renewal.

Although this ceremony is traditionally used for postpartum mothers, it is increasingly being used to promote recovery in war veterans, those with PTSD, other trauma, and anyone who is in need of release, realignment, closure, and healing.

This could be extended to specifically include any person who has been injured by the institution of patriarchy, with its lack of respect, acknowledgement or inclusion of the divine feminine.

We know that in ancient cultures, and still today in various cultures around the world, the power of the feminine is called upon at times of birth, illness, and death. There is an instinctive turning at these liminal times, toward the innate wisdom and knowledge women possess. When in crisis, we long for the guidance, comfort, and support of a mother figure. We long for a strong, wise woman to "make it all better for us," whether we are female, male, or anywhere on the spectrum of humanity.

When a group of women gather together with intent to heal and bless, the power they summon and wield is tangible, as we see from the following interviews with women participants in a Closing of the Bones ceremony facilitated by Sacred Sisters Full Moon Circle:

Interview 1 – Elizabeth:

Q: Did you feel feminine power, love, and healing during this ceremony?

Elizabeth: "Anytime I gather with women for a purpose, feminine power, love, and healing is present. I felt with the Closing of the Bones ceremony, however, something a little more sacred and gentle, almost like a soft goodbye. Don't get me wrong, power was still felt, but in a paradoxical, tender way."

Q: Was this experience beneficial for you as a tool for trauma healing and closure?

Elizabeth: "I feel this experience was beneficial to me as a tool for trauma healing and closure. This ceremony came into my space energetically before I was invited to participate. I had been battling some difficult feelings from all of my miscarriages, sexual abuse and trauma, health issues and body image, expectation of what it means to be a woman (wife, mother, sister, etc.), and all the stress came to a head a couple of weeks before I participated. I had heard of this ceremony before, and it was quite magical when Rebekah created an event for it. It felt right to attend and I'm glad that I did. I felt there was a protected, sweet closure to some of the pain that had resurfaced."

Q: Was this experience healing for your postpartum physical and emotional self?

Elizabeth: "I feel like this ceremony aided in healing me on all the four bodies: physically, mentally, spiritually, and emotionally. There came a bone-deep understanding to the events that happened to me and helped shape the person I am today."

Q: Did you feel a presence like a mother goddess during the ceremony?

Elizabeth: "During this ceremony, I felt a mother goddess presence. I think that's where that powerful, yet gentle essence comes in. I felt safe, protected, and surrounded by my earthly sisters, but also my ancestor angels, especially my mother and maternal grandmother."

Q: Do you feel that this ceremony could be helpful for both women and men to heal the wounds of patriarchy?

Elizabeth: "I feel this ceremony could function as a bridge. I think those still involved in a patriarchal mentality could see the benefits of this ceremony for even just PTSD. I think when there is exposure to healing that is more matriarchal, there is the potential to experience that crossover. But yes, the Closing of the Bones could be a great way for both men and women to heal from any kind of traumas or PTSD that is caused by the patriarchy. I'm grateful that I was able to experience this firsthand, and that we have such an amazing group of women that enjoy gathering to connect and heal."

Interview 2 – Lu:

Q: Did you feel feminine power, love, and healing during this ceremony?

Lu: "It always starts for me during the opening of the circle, when we acknowledge the directions and energies, and then I feel the feminine power all through whatever ceremony we are doing. The Closing of the Bones ceremony was so comforting to me. I felt the feminine energy wrapping around me. After living in an abusive marriage for twenty years and feeling unwanted and unloved, it was so heartwarming to feel the true, real, authentic love of our sisters. As the women placed their hands on me to bless, not only did I feel the warmth and the power spiritually and energetically, I felt tangible love, comforting and healing, that helped my psyche and heart. Through our sisters, I felt the presence of a divine Mother."

Q: Was this experience beneficial for you as a tool for trauma and PTSD closure and healing?

Lu: "For me, this was a tool to help heal trauma and move beyond the debilitation. It picks you up, scoops you up, and you're held in someone's arms. Just the sisterhood and camaraderie of someone being in your corner. The binding, almost swaddling – this particular thing – I felt held together. Because you do feel like you have fallen apart from the trauma on so many levels – the gaslighting, physical, emotional, verbal, and financial abuse, trauma bonding, love bombing if you try to leave. You don't feel like yourself. You feel scattered, and the binding felt like those hands were helping to bring back my wholeness."

Q: Would this experience be healing for postpartum individuals?

Lu: "On a postpartum level, since my daughter just gave birth at the end of August, I wish she could experience this kind of tribal support. As a new mom you can feel strung out. I wish my daughter could experience this sisterhood of love."

Q: Do you feel that this ceremony could be helpful for both women and men to heal the wounds of patriarchy?

Lu: "In my opinion, I think it would be helpful for men to experience this too. The more that men can be introduced and encouraged to nurture their feminine side the better off society is."

In my own experience as a single woman and mother, women's circles in general and the Closing of the Bones ceremony in particular, have helped me to heal from my own wounds caused by patriarchy. The religion in which I was raised, sings a hymn by Eliza R. Snow which has the line, "Truth is reason, truth eternal, tells me I've a Mother there." Although the church of my childhood and younger life does acknowledge the existence of a "Mother in Heaven," it is frowned upon if she is explored too much, or prayed to. If members have too many public questions to ask, or too much to say about a Heavenly Mother, they could face church censure or even excommunication.

As a child I wasn't consciously aware of feeling the lack of a divine feminine presence, likely because we did sing the Eliza R. Snow hymn quite often, because my own mother was a strong positive presence in my life, and because it was clear that my father respected her greatly. However, in my adult life, during a long, abusive marriage, I did become aware of a huge lack, and felt the need to fully include the presence of the divine feminine in every aspect of my life. During the last six years, as I have turned to women's spirituality and walked this path on an ever-deepening level, I have encountered many beautiful, healing ideas, rituals, and ceremonies, such as the Closing of the Bones, that have absolutely filled a longing and a need I didn't know I had. Freeing myself from the constrictions and limitations of patriarchy by fully acknowledging the goddess in all her manifestations. Through facilitating women's circles and rituals has brought me deep fulfillment, healing, and joy.

Preparation for the Closing of the Bones Ceremony

If you wish to facilitate your own Closing of the Bones ceremony, it is important to remember and to clearly acknowledge that this is an indigenous practice. If you are able to receive training or guidance from a Latina woman, or a woman of Indonesian, or Moroccan descent who has knowledge of this ceremony, that would be wonderful. There are authentic videos available online that will also be helpful to you.

You will need the Following Supplies:

- Five long wide rebozo, manta, or other scarves
- A yoga mat or foam pad
- Two pillows
- Two blankets
- A basin for bathing feet
- Fresh washcloths and towels for each participant
- Heated water
- Herbs for special tea and foot bathing
- Bone broth

Recipe for Special Closing of the Bones Tea:

This recipe is courtesy of Sariah A. Price, a Utah-based doula, who learned both recipe and ceremony technique from her Mexican grandmother, a Curandera.

- 1 t. calendula
- 1 t. chamomile
- 1 t. dandelion leaf
- 1 t. lemon grass
- 1 t. raspberry leaf
- ½ t. rosemary
- ¼ t. cumin

Make individual take-home tea bags for each participant, as well as having enough tea brewed for everyone attending your ceremony to drink afterwards. Sprinkle a little of these herbs in each fresh foot bath.

How to Conduct the Ceremony:

Begin your circle by creating a peaceful, sacred space.

- First, smudge with a bundle of thyme, rosemary, lavender, or juniper to purify both space and individual.
- Hold hands in a circle and together take three deep breaths, inhaling to the count of four, and exhaling to the count of four to expel the stresses of the day.
- Take turns going around the circle with each participant introducing herself and her matrilineal line, example: "I am Jane, daughter of Lucy, granddaughter of Helen and Susan."
- Mark the four directions with their corresponding elements and begin the main ceremony.
- Briefly explain the origin and purpose of the ceremony.
- Perform the bathing of the feet, gentle healing touch to head and shoulders, and silent blessing for the first, and then subsequent recipient(s).

- The recipient then lies upon the mat for the rebozo massage with the scarves. Sisters of the circle gather around her.
- After the special realigning massage, the participant is bound with the scarves upon vital points of the body. The sisters in your circle then silently bless her with healing hands, and at this point a special song (found below) is sung by all but the recipient.
- After singing the song three times, slowly unwrap the recipient and help her to rise.
- Give the recipient warm bone broth and the special herbal tea.
- Repeat until every person in your circle has received the closure.

Closing of the Bones Song:

Tierra mi cuerpo	(Earth my body)
Agua mi sangre	(Water my blood)
Aire mi aliento	(Air my breath)
Y fuego mi espiritu	(And Fire my spirit)

With the exception of this song, everything is done in silence so all present can meditate and connect to spirit and their own inner selves.

How to Perform a Rebozo Massage:

- As the recipient lies on the spread out scarf, gently lift her using each side of the scarf. It is helpful to have a partner on the other side of the scarf to coordinate with you, but not necessary.
- Slightly pull to gently stretch the spine.
- Gently shake.
- Gently roll from side to side.
- Lower
- Bind
- Bless and sing.
- Unwrap and release.

Bright Blessings to you as you practice and perform this uplifting, healing Closing of the Bones ceremony for your circle of loved ones!

Poem by Rebekah Myers, copyright © by Rebekah Myers, November 19th, 2018

Essay copyright © by Rebekah Myers, December 8th, 2021

Photo Credits: Elizabeth Harris Denis and Rebekah Myers

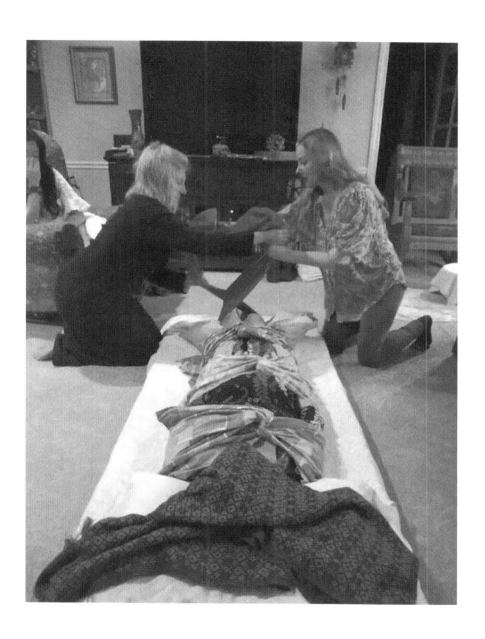

285

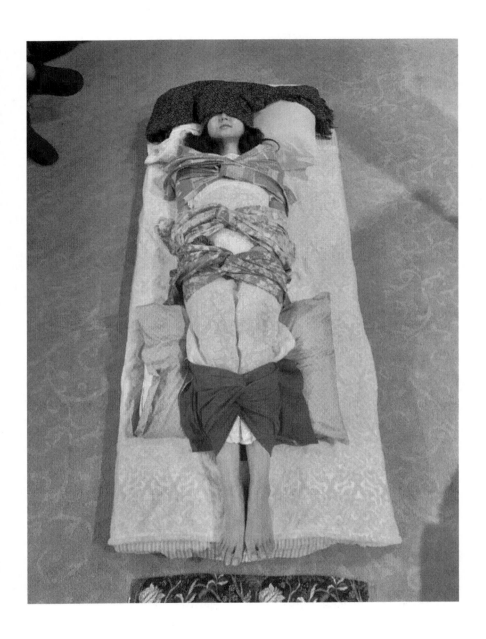

Conclusion
Trista Hendren

I like to think that Goddess has a sense of humor.

She tends to show up for me that way anyway, in Her various and glorious forms.

I am a person who likes to laugh. As someone who grew up as an unhappy child, I take my joy very seriously now.

Anything that stands in the way of my peace of mind or my family's happiness and well-being has to go.

As we wrapped up this book in final editing, I went through another Dark Night of the Soul—except that the 'night' lasted several months.

It brought back PTSD stemming from sexual trauma and my utter lack of agency as a child. I could barely brush my teeth or take my vitamins without gagging.

Like my earlier sexual trauma, I buried it deep and mostly kept it to myself.

I went into hibernation mode and slept a lot. My dreams were often terrifying, but I knew I had to work through them.

I began to feel better as I let people back in. Being deeply heard is tremendously healing. None of us were meant to carry so many burdens. Every time we let go of something that was not meant for us to hold on to, we are healing our little part of the world.

I was not able to let it all go until I wailed it all out in heavy sobs to a dear old friend.

287

I needed to be heard.

And then I could move on. And heal.

Clarissa Pinkola Estés wrote: "Tears are a river that takes you somewhere. Weeping creates a river around the boat that carries your soul-life. Tears lift your boat off the rocks, off dry ground, carrying it downriver to someplace better." I believe in the deep healing power of tears. I have seen the miracles of wailing.

These COVID years have been rough on everyone. Not being able to meet regularly (or at all) in person is not how humans were meant to live. Women need our sisters. We need our circles. We need our rituals and our communities.

Take heart: They will come back.

Until then, we must all continue to do the best we can within the confines imposed on us.

This book was exactly the thing I needed at this point in my life. I had not planned it that way. I thought it would be a book to help *other* people.

And yet, so many of the stories resonated deeply. So many of the rituals and suggestions were deeply helpful in yet another round of my healing journey.

Healing, I have come to accept, is not a one and done. I have returned to wounds many times that I thought I had worked through. Laura Davis reminds us:

> "The healing process is best described as a spiral. Survivors go through the stages once, sometimes many times; sometimes in one order, sometimes in another. Each time they hit a

stage again, they move up the spiral: they can integrate new information and a broader range of feelings, utilize more resources, take better care of themselves, and make deeper changes."[50]

This anthology is a gift that you can come back to again and again. If something does not resonate your first read through, it may later. I often find that some of my favorite books and passages were ones that I could not focus on initially.

I was not ready for the message.

I have often felt like healing my trauma has been like peeling off layers that no longer fit. I have learned to embrace the ease in which snakes shed their skins. It doesn't always have to be as difficult as we make it.

Be gentle with yourself. You can come back to the process at your leisure. There is no rushing in healing. There is no shame in needing time—and in not having everything perfectly together. Many of us who have been shattered the most also contain a deeper capacity for joy. Kahlil Gibran wrote:

> "Your joy is your sorrow unmasked. And the selfsame well from which your laughter rises was oftentimes filled with your tears. And how else can it be? The deeper that sorrow carves into your being, the more joy you can contain."[51]

Whatever your path, I hope you know that you deserve to find healing—and immense joy. So, give yourself a big hug. You have been through a lot—and your life was meant to be celebrated.

---

50 Davis, Laura. *Allies in Healing: When the Person You Love Was Sexually Abused as a Child.* William Morrow Paperbacks; 1st edition, 1991.
51 Gibran, Kahlil. *The Prophet.* Knopf; 1923.

Big Hug
Leticia Banegas

Additional Reading and Resources

Irene Lyon's work has been helpful to many. Check out her YouTube channel, particularly these videos: "The burden of childhood trauma and how to lift it" and "How to come out of a chronic freeze response after repeated stress & trauma." https://irenelyon.com/

Aphrodite's Magic: Celebrate and Heal Your Sexuality – Jane Meredith

Blood and Honey: The Secret Herstory of Women: South Slavic Women's Experiences in a World of Modern-day Territorial Warfare – Danica Anderson PhD,

Breaking Down the Wall of Silence: The Liberating Experience of Facing Painful Truth – Alice Miller

Call of the Wild: How We Heal Trauma, Awaken Our Own Power, and Use It For Good – Kimberly Ann Johnson

Complex PTSD: From Surviving to Thriving: A GUIDE AND MAP FOR RECOVERING FROM CHILDHOOD TRAUMA – Pete Walker

Dance of Psyche: Rhythm of Consciousness – Dr. Christina T. Campbell

In an Unspoken Voice: How the Body Releases Trauma and Restores Goodness – Peter A. Levine and Gabor Maté MD

Nurturing Resilience: Helping Clients Move Forward from Developmental Trauma—An Integrative Somatic Approach – Kathy L. Kain and Stephen J. Terrell

Patriarchy Stress Disorder: the Invisible Inner Barrier to Women's Happiness and Fulfillment – Dr. Valerie Rein

Trauma and Recovery: The Aftermath of Violence—from Domestic Abuse to Political Terror – Judith Herman, M.D.

The Body Keeps the Score: Brain, Mind, and Body in the Healing of Trauma – Bessel van der Kolk, M.D.

The Courage to Heal: A Guide for Women Survivors of Child Sexual Abuse – Ellen Bass and Laura Davis

Waking the Tiger: Healing Trauma: The Innate Capacity to Transform Overwhelming Experiences – Peter A. Levine and Ann Frederick

When the Body Says No: Understanding the Stress-Disease Connection – Gabor Mate, M.D.

You Can Heal Your Life – Louise Hay

Your Life After Trauma: Powerful Practices to Reclaim Your Identity – Michelle Rosenthal

List of Contributors

Alissa DeLaFuente lives and works in the Pacific Northwest. Her creative work has appeared in scientific and literary journals, including *Oyster River Pages, Photonics Focus, Gold Man Review*, and in two Girl God anthologies titled *Warrior Queen: Answering the Call of the Morrigan* and *Just as I Am: Hymns Affirming the Divine Female.* She regularly serves as a prose judge for the International Latino Book Awards. Visit her at www.alissadelafuente.com to learn more.

Alorah Welti is a second-generation goddess worshipper, artist, and poet. She is a birthworker living in Berkshire County, Massachusetts.

Amber R. Balk, Ph.D. carries forth an ancestral blend of southeastern Native North American Mississippian heritage combined with English, Irish, and Welsh European American lineage. She holds a MA in Women's Spirituality and a Ph.D. in Transpersonal Psychology, both from the Institute of Transpersonal Psychology in Palo Alto, California. Amber collaborates with individuals and groups providing a range of psychospiritual opportunities that include astrology, dreamwork, expanded states of consciousness, spiritual community action, and visits to sacred sites across the planet.

See transpersonalsessions.com for more information on her offerings. Amber can be contacted at dr.amberbalk@gmail.com and is also on Instagram @transpersonalsessions. She spends her days utterly enchanted by the Pacific Northwest, baffled and amazed by her teenage daughter, and lovingly immersed in creating a forthcoming series of spiritual fantasy sci-fi novels.

Poet, performer, and teacher **Annie Finch** is the author of a dozen books including *The Poetry Witch Little Book of Spells, Eve, A Poet's Craft*, and the epic poem on abortion *Among the*

Goddesses, which received the Sarasvati Award from ASWM. Her eight edited books include *Choice Words: Writers on Abortion*, the first major literary anthology on abortion. She holds a Ph.D. from Stanford University and descends from witches imprisoned in the Salem Witch Trials. Annie has taught widely and performs through Poetry Witch Ritual Theater.

She teaches classes in poetry, meter, witchery, and her original transformative teaching, The Magic of Rhythmically Writing, at PoetryWitchCommunity.org. You can find Annie on Twitter: @poetrywitch and Instagram: @thepoetrywitch.

Arlene Bailey is a visionary artist and author working in the realm of the Sacred Female in all her many visages. Arlene's paintings and poetry/prose reflect the raw, visceral and sacred wild in all women, while challenging and questioning everything we know to be true about *the who* of who we are as women walking in this time.

Through her magical weavings in word and paint—and, drawing on her trainings and skills as an Ordained Priestess, Women's Mysteries Facilitator, Wise Woman Herbalist, Energy Medicine Practitioner and Retired Anthropologist—Arlene invites women to step into personal sovereignty as they listen to their ancient memories and voice of their soul.

Published in several Girl God Books' anthologies, Arlene is also a monthly contributor to *Return to Mago* E-Magazine and has writings in two forthcoming Mago anthologies. Her work can also be found on *The Sacred Wild*, a page on Facebook about re-wilding woman's soul.

Along with her partner and five cats, this Wild Crone lives on 18 acres of deep woods and quartz outcroppings in the Uwharrie Mountains of North Carolina, USA.

www.facebook.com/sacredwildstudio
www.instagram.com/arlenebaileyartist

Arna Baartz is a painter, writer/poet, martial artist, educator and mother to eight fantastic children. She has been expressing herself creatively for more than 40 years and finds it to be her favourite way of exploring her inner being enough to evolve positively in an externally-focused world. Arna's artistic and literary expression is her creative perspective of the stories she observes playing out around her. Claims to fame: Arna has been selected for major art prizes and won a number of awards, published many books, and— (her favourite) was being used as a 'paintbrush' at the age of two by well-known Australian artist John Olsen. Arna lives and works from her bush studio in the Northern Rivers, NSW Australia. Her website is arnabaartz.com.au.

Barbara C. Daughter – artist, author, teacher, and spiritual guide – centers love in her being-ness, bringing that intention to all she encounters on many paths. Restoring sovereignty to women via our connections to each other, Mother Earth and ancestral Motherlines are the primary rituals through which she develops this deepening wisdom.

Barbara works primarily in acrylics, creating large-scale "magical realism" paintings of imaginal, mythical women. Since childhood, she has created with her hands, from fiber arts to jewelry-making. She continues to study with Shiloh Sophia, internationally renowned artist and founder of Intentional Creativity®.

Barbara's work speaks to the deep need for women to see themselves as sacred beings, connected to Mother Earth, and to her Sacred Mysteries which emanate from myths and cultural traditions from around the world.

As an Intentional Creativity Artist & Teacher and Spiritual Life Coach, Barbara guides women on journeys to their own inner wisdom.

Barbara O'Meara is a professional visual artist, art activist, published writer & co-editor of 'Soul Seers Irish Anthology of Celtic Shamanism'. With 20 Solo Exhibitions including 'B.O.R.N. -Babies of Ravaged Nations'. International juried shows include ASWM 'Wisdom Across the Ages', Lockhart Gallery New York 'Contemporary Irish Art' & 'Herstory' Brigid's of the World & Black Lives Matter. Community Arts include 'Stitched With Love' Tuam Baby Blanket laid out onsite at the Mother & Child Institution by survivors & families, shown at KOLO International Women's Non Killing Cross Borders Summit in Sarajevo & held by Bosnian women war survivors. 'Sort Our Smears' Campaign at 'Festival of FeminismS'. 'Home Words Bound' publication with National Collective of Community Based Women's Networks where her paintings accompany writing by women about the Pandemic. She is continually developing empowering women's 'Art as Activism' projects. Her artwork & writing feature in several Girl God Books: She recently illustrated *My Name is Brigid* launched on Brigid's Day by Girl God Books www.barbaraomearaartist.com

C. Abigail Pingree spent the first seven years of her life in a primarily off-grid hippie commune in the lush green foothills of Western Washington. These early experiences helped shape a curious approach to the world, and contributed to her strong connection with nature.

She is currently a poet, author, mother, death doula, and Registered Nurse.

She has made friends with her own experiences of addiction and inauthenticity by simply telling her truth. She now seeks an authentic life, whatever that means.

Caroline Selles is a veterinarian, reiki practitioner, poet and painter. A self-taught intuitive artist, Caroline began painting as a way of healing thru decades of physical and emotional trauma and illness. What began as a meditative practice with a desire to see more diversity of form and culture in art, has become a spiritual and healing practice and the pathway to finding Goddess and reclaiming her own suppressed cultural inheritance and feminine power. Essential themes of her art and poems include reclaiming female empowerment, female divinity and diversity, integration after trauma and nature as goddess imagery. Born in Valencia, Spain, she currently resides in the United States. She can be found on social media as @thegoddesswithinart or at https://thegoddesswithinart.square.site.

Rev. Christian Ortiz, Ph.D.
Psychologist (CUCH)
Specialist in Religious Studies (ULC)
Priest of the Goddess
Member of the Fraternity of the Goddess

Certified Specialist in Violence Prevention and Care (UCC - ELPAC), coordinator of the C. G. Jung deep psychology study circle from Mexico, member of the C. G. Jung Foundation and the Ibero-American Transpersonal Association.

Host of "SABER SANAR" podcast and Circle Sanctuary Network Podcasts. He currently coordinates psychoeducational care programs for the Awakened Men-Masculinities organization and collaborates with academic institutions on issues of culture of peace.

Claire Dorey
Goldsmiths: BA Hons Fine Art.
Main Employment: Journalist and Creative, UK and overseas.
Artist: Most notable group show; Pillow Talk at the Tate Modern. Included in the Pillow Talk Book.

Curator: 3 x grass roots SLWA exhibitions and educational events on the subject of Female Empowerment, showcasing female artists, academic speeches and local musicians. Silence Is Over – Raising awareness on violence towards women; Ex Voto –

Existential Mexican Art Therapy; Heo - Female empowerment in the self-portrait.

Extra study: Suppressed Female History: History of the Goddess; Accessing Creative Wisdom; Sound and Breath Work; Reiki Master; Colour Therapy; Hand Mudras; Reflexology; Sculpture. Teaching Workshops: Sculpture and Drawing.

Dawn Perez is a writer, mother, and feminist. Formerly, she was a music teacher in the public schools for ten years. She lives in New Mexico with her amazing husband and two sons, who are the joy of her life. When she's not writing, she spends her time hiking, singing, and rock climbing. You can read more of her work at wildsimplejoy.com, which focuses on healing our bodies, minds, and spirits as women and mothers.

Deborah A. Meyerriecks is a retired NYC*EMS Lieutenant from the NYC Fire Department. A self-dedicated Witch and acting community priestess she has offered guidance and spiritual counseling to support others while they discover their own personal right path. Since responding to the Call of The Morrigan and becoming Her priest, she found her self-healing and shadow work have been exponentially more productive as she navigates her personal lessons this live has to offer. Deborah's first manuscript was recently completed and although still in editing, she is excited for the upcoming release of "Macha and the Medic: Service and Priesthood on the Frontlines of Life."

Dr. Denise Renye is a licensed clinical psychologist, certified sexologist, executive consultant and coach, certified yoga therapist, and psychedelic integrationist. She has specialized training in and has worked directly with people in the areas of sexuality, relationships, states of consciousness, psychedelic integration and intimacy. She holds a Master's degree in Human Sexuality from Widener University (Philadelphia), as well as a Master's degree and a Doctoral degree in Clinical Psychology from the California Institute of Integral Studies (San Francisco). Dr. Denise is certified as a sexologist through the American College of Sexologists. She was in the first cohort to graduate from the Center for Psychedelic Therapies and Research (CPTR) at CIIS and provides psychedelic integration individually and in group settings, utilizing trauma-informed and somatics approaches. She has studied embodied spiritual practices nationally and internationally through research and experiential learning and has conducted and published research on embodied psycho-spirituality.

Dona Tumacder-Esteban, from the Philippines, braids together Embodiment practices, Energy Management for high performing organizations, and an approach to Women's Well-being and Leadership that honor our deep Feminine Energy Cycle, Womb Wisdom, Indigenous roots, and earth-based practices. As an ancestor to future generations, Dona's present moment purpose is to ignite, catalyze, and realize a flourishing inner and outer world that is loving, truthful, and grounded in serving our innate Wholeness and Oneness, both as individuals and as a global community. She shares extensively on both live and online platforms through workshops, Talking Circles, women's circles, and one-on-one mentoring in Asia Pacific and Europe. Dona dedicates her inner and outer work to her daughter, Carmen. www.innermoonwellbeing.com IG @innermoonwellbeing

Donna Gerrard is an initiated Priestess of Brighde-Brigantia, of the Rose lineage, and of the Sacred Bee. Healing the witch wound is very dear to her heart, her direct maternal line being from Pendle, Lancashire, location of the biggest witch trial in English history. Donna is also a poet and a long time practitioner and teacher of yoga: her classes often interweave poetry and the spirituality of these other ancient traditions with that of yoga, in a way that passionately communicates the transformative power of these ancient Goddess traditions in a modern context. donnagerrard.com

D'vorah J. Grenn, Ph.D., Kohenet, is Founding Director, The Lilith Institute (1997). She co-directed the former Women's Spirituality MA Program at Institute of Transpersonal Psychology/Sofia University, and founded Mishkan Shekhinah, a movable sanctuary honoring the Sacred Feminine in all traditions. D'vorah leads the Institute's Lilith's Fire Circle and other programs, and also serves as a spiritual mentor and guide. Her *Talking To Goddess* anthology includes sacred writings of 72 women from 25 spiritual traditions. Her dissertation, "For She Is A Tree of Life: Shared Roots Connecting Women to Deity" studied beliefs and rituals among South African Lemba Jewish women. Other publications include *Lilith's Fire: Reclaiming our Sacred Lifeforce;* "The *Kohanot*: Keepers of the Flame", in *Stepping into Ourselves: An Anthology of Writing on Priestesses (Key & Cant); and the Jewish priestess and Lilith entries in the Encyclopedia of Women in World Religions (de-Gaia).*

Contact info: dvorah@lilithinstitute.com; @lilithinstitute on Instagram.

Edy Levin uses her artistic tools to yield abstractions, mandalas, horses, and still-life paintings. Her work is inspired by moon phases, Goddess archetypes, animal guides, and the labyrinthine path that unfolds before her. She began her artistic journey in South Carolina where she was influenced by her grandmother, a prolific painter, and her mother, a gifted pianist. After she received a B.A. in studio art from Hollins University and an M.F.A. in painting from Indiana University, Edy moved to Los Angeles, where she began teaching at Brentwood School. For over two decades, Edy has been developing an interdisciplinary style that expresses a pantheistic empathy with nature and, more specifically, an impassioned connection to horses and rural landscapes. She often finds herself reconciling the differences and highlighting the similarities between her rural Southern roots and the metropolitan behemoth she now calls home. Find her work at edymade.com and @edymadecreations on IG.

Ellie Lieberman works with the fairies on her handmade business, Acorn Tops, when not writing and illustrating. Her writing includes two children's book series, short stories, and a novel that was fourteen years in the making. An avid reader with a bedroom that looks like a mini library, Ellie is a lover of all things purple and glittery, basset hound, squirrel, gardening, and milk chocolate, with a slight fried rice obsession. She can be found across social media on Facebook, Twitter, Tumblr, Instagram, and Amazon.

Helena Anderson is a Mother, partner, and friend who cooks with herbs and heals with love. Her secret passions include casting spells, healing the Patriarchy, moving pens over paper, and dancing with all the magical creatures that come to her parties. She holds a degree in Psychology but she tries not to let that get in her way too much. She lives in a caravan in the jungle with Rainforest Ryan (her half human half crocodile husband of 15 years) where together, they unschool their wild pirate son Captain Mikey.

For the past two decades, **Jen Abha** has been called to return to her roots. Honing her skills as a Somatic Educator practicing Trauma Informed Care, Body Lover Extraordinaire, Shakti Queen, Medicinal and Kitchen Herbalist, Yoga Therapist, Energy Healing Practitioner, Naturopath in training, believer in matrilineal ways of living and loving through her attached Mothering, embodying authenticity. Passionate about cultivating growth mindsets, and building healthy relationships by doing the inner work, being asked for self and the collective. Refining awareness to embody the mindful high road of loving boundaries, interconnected, through the divine connection of intuition.

May we all live a life of Love, Light and Levity – infinitely.

In her name.

Kaia Tingley is a writer, artist, podcaster, digital strategy nerd, and sometimes hot-tempered supernova with a wild, free soul. You can find her on Instagram or on LinkedIn.
https://www.instagram.com/muse.of.creativity
https://www.linkedin.com/in/kaiamaeve

Karen Ward PhD is a Shamanic Therapist, Supervisor and Teacher. Trained in the Celtic lineage and Druidic traditions, she co-founded and runs the Slí An Chroí School of Irish Celtic Shamanism with her husband John Cantwell. Her very popular Moon Mná (Gaelic for Moon Women), the women's section, offers online courses incorporating Rite of Passage Ceremonies inspired by the archetypal energies of the Irish Goddesses. Karen is author of renowned book *Change a Little to Change a Lot* (2009), co-editor of *Soul Seers – an Irish Anthology of Celtic Shamanism* (2019) and the annual *Moon Mná Diary-Journal* (2017) to date. She is a Counselling Psychotherapist and Supervisor based at her Dublin Clinic since 1997, leading workshops countrywide and abroad to teach her Energy Therapy technique based on Celtic Shamanism to fellow health practitioners. She is honoured to have co-rediscovered the Brigid's Way Celtic Pilgrimage in 2012.
www.slianchroi.ie www.moonmna.ie
www.drkarenwardtherapist.ie

Kathy Barenskie is labelled in the 'Medical Model' of diagnostic terms, to be an Autistic. This naive, trusting way of 'Being' has resulted in having faced many difficult experiences in her life. Yet also, it has afforded her many strengths. In reality, she has been blessed with a great empathy and sensitivity. She is a Mother of three grown-up wonderful children.

Her career path has flowed along the path of discovery of herself and being in the service of others: Registered State General Nurse, Accredited Psychodynamic Therapist, Reiki Master, Dru Yoga Teacher, Yoga Meditation Teacher, Laughter Yoga Leader. Now, in her 50s, she practices a Core Shamanism and is also a certified

Shamanic Counsellor. As a special interest, Kathy crafts tools of power—Rattles, Snake Charms, Spells, Totems with Crystals and Stones.

Kat Shaw prides herself on breaking through the stereotypical views of beauty that have been cast upon society by the media, having made her name painting the glorious reality that is a woman's body.

Her nude studies of real women garnered unprecedented popularity within only a few short months, as women were crying out for themselves to be portrayed in art, rather than the airbrushed images of the perfection of the female form that are so rife in today's culture.

After graduating with a fine art degree, Kat achieved a successful full-time teaching career for 14 years, and continues to teach art part-time whilst passionately pursuing her mission of world domination by empowering as many women as possible to reach their fullest potential by embracing their bodies and loving themselves wholeheartedly.

Kat spreads her inspirational magic through her artwork, her Wellbeing business "Fabulously Imperfect", and her dedication to Goddess energy.

Reiki is a huge part of her life, and as a Reiki Master, Kat is committed to sharing Reiki, teaching Usui, Angelic and Karuna Reiki, and channelling Reiki energy through her artwork to uplift and heal.

As a Sister of Avalon, Kat also works directly with her Goddess consciousness, connecting to Goddess and Priestess energy and translating it into Divine Feminine infused paintings to inspire women and spread Goddess love.

Kat is also mum to a gorgeous teenage daughter, a belly dancer and an avid pioneer to improve the lives of rescue animals.

Katrina Stadler is an artist who lives in Christchurch and is currently studying Bachelor of Design (Applied Visual Arts) at Ara Institute of Canterbury. She is inspired by the work of many women artists, particularly when they are making a statement about the experience of living in a woman's body or aspects of a woman's inner or outer life. Katrina is a Art of Allowing facilitator, and has facilitated women's painting and creativity workshops. Her paintings start out as play on the canvas and then intuitively seeing and feeling what is calling to come forth, and mostly that has been feminine forms.

2020 – 2021 Bachelor of Design (Applied Visual Arts)
2020 – Year 1 Contextual Studies prize
2020 – Solo exhibition *The Creatrix*. Methven Memorial Hall. Canterbury
2018 – Joint exhibition *Muses and Madonnas, The Feminine as Creatrix*. Pumanawa Gallery Christchurch Arts Centre.
2017-2019 – Painting and creativity workshop facilitator
2017 – Certified Art of Allowing facilitator

Her website is www.katrinaleah.com.

Kay Louise Aldred writes and edits for Girl God Books. She has contributed to the Girl God Anthologies *Warrior Queen, Answering the Call of the Morrigan, In Defiance of Oppression - The Legacy of Boudicca and Just as I am - Hymns Affirming the Divine Female*. Kay will also feature in the Girl God Anthology *Songs of Solstice - Goddess Carols* scheduled for publication in 2022. Currently she is co-editing the four upcoming Girl God Anthologies: *Re-Membering with Goddess: Healing the Patriarchal Perpetuation of Trauma, The Crone Initiation and Invitation: Women speak on the Menopause Journey, Rainbow Goddess - Celebrating Neurodiversity* and *Pain Perspectives: Finding Meaning in the Fire*. Scheduled publication for these books is 2022/2023. In addition, Kay is writing her own books. *Mentorship of Goddess: Growing Sacred Womanhood* will be published June 2022 and *Making Love with the Divine: Sacred,*

Ecstatic, Erotic Experiences is scheduled for February 2023. Finally, Kay and her husband Dan Aldred, are co-authoring a book together, *Embodied Education*, which will be available June 2023.

Leticia Banegas is a Honduran fine arts figurative painter. Art has been a passion for her for as long as she can remember. Her work is the representation of a world that exists somewhere between heaven and earth. When she paints, she sees these women. She sees them walking like they are underwater with their hair flowing in slow motion. They exist, she sees them. It's a magical realm that most of us can't see, but that doesn't mean it doesn't exist. What inspires her are the women in her family through generations. Their stories are so rich, complex and some of them almost surreal. She tries to create a "world" populated by the magical presence of these women.

Leticia also likes to work with female archetypes, representing them with her personal stamp.

Her work can be found at: https://www.leticiabanegasart.net/
https://www.facebook.com/leticiabanegasgomez
https://www.instagram.com/leticia.banegasart/

Liz Darling is a visual artist known for cosmic, organic paintings that often feature fungi, lunar imagery, and the female body. With a precise, organized approach and a personal emphasis on process and exploration, Liz uses watercolor, ink, and various other media to engage the intersection of magic, nature, the divine feminine, and the inner child. Liz exhibits her work in various gallery shows, festivals, markets, and publications. She is a member of the Joplin Regional Artists' Coalition, a frequent contributor to the *We'Moon* astrological datebook, and her work appears on the film sets of the HBO show *Mrs. Fletcher* and Hulu's *Sex Appeal*. In addition to making art, she enjoys hiking, documenting beautiful things in nature, traveling with her family, playing music, and walking her beloved dog, Oro. Liz lives and works in Pittsburg, KS, surrounded by the prairie and wide Kansas sky.

Lori Santo is a highly sensitive, creative empath. She is a fearless, courageous, raw artist. She is a trauma-informed, Soul-searing poetess who transmits tremendous energy to support women who have endured severe abuse. Lori is a Divine, highly artistic storyteller who navigates the underworld and the powerful emotional storms with enchantment, sorcery, sophistication and precision.

Through written and live storytelling coupled with performance art, Lori coaches and supports highly sensitive, empathic, creative women who have experienced radical abuse and have not yet owned or fully expressed their personal story passionately. Her art, and life's work, facilitate the deep alchemy of sacred, compassionate healing through artistic alchemy, witnessing and celebration.

Louise M Hewett engages in a strange and sometimes slow motion dance of writing, art, mothering, dreaming, and learning about the maternal gift paradigm. She has written five out of seven novels in the Pictish Spirit series, an adventure in love and intimacy shaped with Goddess feminism, hopes for partnership society beyond patriarchy, and the beneficial practise of risking creativity. She hopes to live long enough to see the world change and women freed from cycles of violence and subjugation.

Dr Lynne Sedgmore CBE is a Priestess of Avalon, Poetess, retired Chief Executive, soul coach and Priestess healer. She is founder and tutor of the Goddess Luminary Leadership Wheel trainings, a unique combination of liberating leadership, feminism and Goddess spirituality offered through the Glastonbury Goddess Temple. Her new book, *The Goddess Luminary Leadership Wheel,* was published by John Hunt, Changemakers Imprint, in 2022. Lynne has spent her professional career teaching and leading in the UK Further Education sector. Her roles included CEO of 157 Group, Chief Executive of the national Centre for Excellence in Leadership, and Principal of Guildford College.

Her three poetry collections are *Enlivenment* (Chrysalis Press 2013), *Healing through the Goddess* (TheaSpeaks Press 2017) and *Crone* (TheaSpeaks Press 2019). She has published a range of articles on spirituality and leadership.

She has 3 daughters and 2 granddaughters and lives in Glastonbury UK.

Lindsay goes by the Nom de Plume '**M^h**'; Mind 'to the power of' the Heart. A truth-seeking, soul-searching storyteller. A deeply rooted practical psycho-spiritual Healer + Lover + Warrior and mind-body-soul integrating anarcha-feminist, amongst many other indefinable droplets of her ever flowing and evolving personhood.

She is the Creatrix of the Poetry anthology *What my body knew* (2020) as well as the preceding chapbooks, *Of Lilith and Delilah* and *Human Nature* together with many other workbooks and creations in motion.

Maureen Owen – PCC, MDOT Transformational Coach, and Facilitator

Clients describe Maureen as insightful, committed to genuine partnership, kind, ruthlessly non-judgemental and having a remarkable ability to help others think outside their own perspective.

Maureen believes that we have a choice about how we respond and how we turn up in the world, no matter what circumstance we find ourselves in. She is devoted to supporting people to do just that whilst bringing the best of themselves forth.

Maureen has over 25 years' experience working with human dynamics. Her work is focused on supporting leaders navigate leadership challenges in the face of uncertainty.

Committed to fostering thought-provoking and creative partnerships, Maureen encourages her clients to use the challenges they face as catalysts for growth, and the opportunity to learn, bringing more of themselves and their gifts forward to expand what's possible.

Websites
www.lotusspace.com.au/
www.owenconsultingservices.com.au/

Social Media
www.linkedin.com/in/maureenowen/
https://www.facebook.com/lotusspacewisdom

Megan Welti is an artist, poet and energy worker living in Western Massachusetts with her husband, four children and many fur babies. You can find prints of her original watercolors at redrootrising.squarespace.com

Michelle Bear grew up in the Caribbean, and has been lucky to have visited or lived in many parts of the world. After fifteen moves in twenty-six years, she has finally settled in her forever home in a tiny Colorado mountain town with her family and fur babies. She has attended so many universities that she's lost count, but she does have a couple of degrees. Michelle married her soulmate, Tim, twenty-six years ago, and has successfully raised two empathetic and intelligent sons with him. She is a medically retired critical care nurse who is currently putting her education to use while she slowly repairs the damage racked upon her mind and body by our patriarchally, damaged health care system. Wherever you find Michelle, you'll find her five-pound Service Dog named Bear. Don't let their diminutive sizes fool you, both Michelle and Bear are giant in spirit.

Natalie Celine Couillard is a PSW in a long term care facility caring for seniors. She began writing again after an energy healing by a good friend with the intent to assist her in meditation. She is 50 and single. Writing poetry brings her understanding of who she is, consequently bringing some healing and peace. Her writing journey is in its infancy, and she looks forward to seeing where it takes her.

She has had three poems published so far in *A Headrest for Your Soul, Healing Felines and Femmes* and *Dark Poetry Collection*. Healing and the divine feminine have become an evident theme in her pieces.

Pat Daly is a mother of three daughters and proud grandma. A published author / writer on career and job search issues, Pat lives in Portland, Oregon. She has edited each of the Girl God Books from the beginning.

Rebekah Myers is dedicated to opening doors of understanding on behalf of women everywhere. She is the founder/facilitator of Sacred Sisters Full Moon Circle, which serves as a virtual Facebook and Instagram public page, a private Facebook group for women, and an actual women's circle that meets in-person. For International Women's Day in March of 2018, Rebekah was honored to have been one of five women recognized by KSL as Utah's most inspirational women.

Through her social anthropologist parents, Rebekah spent memorable time with the Iroquois (a matrilineal people) of Six Nations Reserve in Ontario, Canada. This experience significantly informed her life for the good. Rebekah has had a life-long interest in and passion for folklore, mythology, and ancient history, and has spent significant time in these worlds. Although Rebekah formally came later in life to women's spirituality, she has found such fulfillment on this path, that there is no turning back. As a writer, teacher, director, award-winning singer/performer/actress, mother, grandmother, and wedding officiator, Rebekah works to empower, enlighten, and uplift women and their brothers. She knows it is possible to heal the wounds of patriarchy and live with depth, meaning, and joy.

Rita Shahi, M.A. is a priestess of the Goddess, ceremonialist, healer, and bodyworker in the San Francisco Bay Area. Her schedule currently offers womyn-only rituals for the 8 high holydays. Rita received her graduate degree from Sonoma State University in Depth Psychology. Her thesis traces the unfolding of the sacred feminine through remembering her motherline that led her on a pilgrimage to her ancestral motherland in the Balkans along the Adriatic Sea. She is dedicated to the Motherline lineage, raising, and uplifting womyn to know who they are and from where they come as a basis for spiritual growth and living earth traditions. Email: solasb@msn.com; www.solasbrigid.massagetherapy.com; www.sacredhearthgoddesstemple.com. Follow her on Instagram at sacredhearthgoddesstemple.

Roxanne Rhoads is an author, artist, book publicist, and all-around crafty witch. Her books include *Haunted Flint* and *Pumpkins and Party Themes: 50 DIY Designs to Bring Your Halloween Extravaganza to Life*.

She is the owner of Bewitching Book Tours, a virtual book tour and social media marketing company. She operates a Halloween blog — *A Bewitching Guide to Halloween* and sells handcrafted jewelry, art, and home decor through her Etsy store The Bewitching Cauldron.

When not reading or writing, Roxanne loves to craft, plan Halloween adventures, and search for unique vintage finds.

Sharon Smith is a writer, ghost writer, editor, and proofreader with a passion for helping women reconnect with their Authentic Selves and Voices. She loves & honors the Great Mother in all Her many forms, and has a deep connection to Nature. She identifies as a Green Witch and follows an eclectic spiritual path that is a blending of Native American and Celtic Teachings, both in her ancestral line.

Painting is **Sue Ellen Parkinson's** doorway through to understanding the world. Creativity is her form of prayer. When she paints a person, she is honoring that Being. That experience is one of deep connection that brings her into wholeness. That's as important to her as oxygen. Her focus is largely about re-visioning, and celebrating womankind—lifting them up. Exploring the Christian mystics has produced a profound change in her. She has found herself particularly drawn to Mary Magdalene. For her, Magdalene is the archetype who represents All Women who have been inaccurately portrayed in history. It's been a healing experience to restore her identity, and the identity of other great women, to the wise and sovereign beings that she believes they are. In so doing, she has become more empowered herself. www.sueellenparkinson.com

Tasha (Burzynski) Curry is a self-proclaimed loud mouth, dedicated to advocating for women. She was born in the burbs of Chicago, but is up for the sea any day. Tasha is an avid gardener, Disney super fan and single Goddess, raising 3 little rays of light. Along her career journey through social services, she has met one too many girls gravely impacted by toxic masculinity and the intergenerational effects of the patriarchy. Her poem is for 2 of those little girls, ravished by the demons of foster care, to whom she promised to "always be a unicorn." Here's to everyone that has ever grieved the loss of their own power.

Trista Hendren founded Girl God Books in 2011 to support a necessary unraveling of the patriarchal world view of divinity. Her first book—*The Girl God*, a children's picture book—was a response to her own daughter's inability to see herself reflected in God. Since then, she has published more than 40 books by a dozen women from across the globe with help from her family and friends. Originally from Portland, Oregon, she now lives in Bergen, Norway. You can learn more about her projects at www.thegirlgod.com.

Trista's Acknowledgments

I would like to acknowledge my co-editors. My mother, **Pat Daly,** has edited each and every one of my books. There would be no Girl God Books without her enormous contributions. I was thrilled to work with **Kay Louise Aldred** on this project as well—who fast became a sister.

Tremendous gratitude to **Kat Shaw** for allowing us to feature her gorgeous painting as the cover art.

Enormous appreciation to my husband **Anders Løberg**, who prepared the document for printing and helped with website updates. Your love, support and many contributions made this book possible.

My mom and I would also like to acknowledge her wonderful partner, **Rick Weiss,** for being an all-around awesome guy—and helping us with the page numbers.

Lastly, I would like to thank my dear sisters **Tamara Albanna, Susan Morgaine, Desiree Jordan, Jeanette Bjørnsen, Camilla Berge Wolff, Tammy Nedrebø-Skurtveit, Kay Louise Aldred, Sharon Smith, Arlene Bailey** and **Alyscia Cunningham** for always being right there to cheer me on in the spirit of true sisterhood.

Thank you to all our readers and Girl God supporters over the years. We love and appreciate you!

Kay's Acknowledgments

I'd like to thank all the women who are currently raising awareness about the nervous system, impact of trauma and intergenerational patterning. I offer my own personal thanks to **Irene Lyon, Kimberley Ann Johnson** and **Bethany Webster.**

I'm grateful to and for the wisdom of our ancestors, bodies and future generations. May **James, Elizabeth, Archie, Helen, Orla** and **Finn** embody their own truth, the 'mined gold' of our familial lines, and live freely and flourish.

Thank you to all practitioners who support trauma resolution and integration, freeing our Spirit to incarnate back into our body and connecting us to our lifeforce.

Gratitude to **Trista Hendren** for birthing Girl God Books and her tireless trail blazing commitment to woman and the sacred feminine. Thank you for believing in me and your yes.

Huge appreciation to my co-editor **Pat Daly** and to **Kat Shaw** for the magnificent and inspiring cover art.

Thank you to all of those who have walked through this life alongside me, without silencing or looking away when I was in pain, suffering or without hope. Thank you for your Light and loving presence.

And finally huge love and appreciation for my husband **Dan** and his endless curiosity, encouragement and avid engagement with my creativity and passions.

If you enjoyed this book, please consider writing a brief review on Amazon and/or Goodreads.

What's Next?!

The Crone Initiation and Invitation: Women speak on the Menopause Journey – Edited by Kay Louise Aldred, Trista Hendren and Pat Daly

Mentorship with Goddess: Growing Sacred Womanhood – Written by Kay Louise Aldred

Rainbow Goddess – Celebrating Neurodiversity – Edited by Kay Louise Aldred, Trista Hendren and Pat Daly

Making Love with the Divine: Sacred, Ecstatic, Erotic Experiences – Kay Louise Aldred

Pain Perspectives: Finding Meaning in the Fire – Edited by Kay Louise Aldred, Trista Hendren and Pat Daly

Embodied Education – Kay Louise Aldred and Dan Aldred

Songs of Solstice: Goddess Carols – Edited by Trista Hendren, Sharon Smith and Pat Daly

Goddess Chants and Songs Book – Edited by Trista Hendren, Anique Radiant Heart and Pat Daly

Anthologies and children's books on the Black Madonna, Mary Magdalene, Mother Mary, Aradia, Kali, Brigid, Sophia, Spider Woman, Persephone, The Old Antlered One/Ancient Deer Goddess, An' Cailleach and Hecate are also in the works.

Details to be announced.

http://thegirlgod.com/publishing.php